Between The
Rock
and   a
Hard
Place

*Adventuring into the
life of Jesus of Nazareth*

James S. Woodroof

The Bible House, Inc.
901 S. Main • P. O. Box 1108
Searcy, Arkansas 72143
Ph. 501-268-9885

Published by
The Bible House
Searcy, AR 72143

Printed by
Gospel Light Publishing Company
Delight, AR

Scripture taken from the *Holy Bible, New International Version.* Copyright c 1973, 1978, 1984 by International Bible Society. Used by permission.

ISBN: 0-9622649-0-3

Acknowledgements

This book, more than any other I have written, has placed the author in debt to a host of helpers — believers and skeptics alike. Grammarians, logicians, theologians, historians and the man and woman on the street have read critically this material and have contributed to its accuracy and readability. To them I am greatly indebted.

Among those who have contributed most significantly is my oldest son, Tim, upon whom I depended heavily for critical analysis. As the various editions of the typescript would come limping back to me bleeding with red pencil marks, I was reminded of the hours Tim and I often spent during his teen years debating various issues, hearing and presenting evidence and counter-evidence on themes that seemed important to a young man. He has more than repaid those long hours with the labor he invested in this present work.

Thanks to Gayle Erwin, author of *The Jesus Style,* for his reading of the typescript and for his encouragement. Appreciation is expressed to my son, David, for his practical advice regarding readability of the text. I mention also Alex Loan, Charles Adams, Ray Lang and Chuck Hatherill and a host of encouragers including Terry Smith, my enthusiast, and Carl and Katherina Beavers for their support during the writing of the text. I express appreciation also to my wife, Louine, who bore with me through the long hours I spent over the keyboard of the computer. Thanks to Joe Buser for his usual faithful job of "subliminal" proofing.

Special appreciation is due Prof. F. F. Bruce, once again, for his encouragement from the very beginning of the project, and F. Lagard Smith, author of the *Narrated Bible,* for writing the foreword.

I am indebted also to the libraries of Harvard University for allowing access to the materials necessary to document this work.

To all who had any part in bringing this project to fruition I express appreciation.

James S. Woodroof

Table of Contents

Foreword

In an age when many would not give even the slightest credibility to the person of Jesus of Nazareth, comes James Woodroof's book asking two crucial questions: "Is Jesus merely a legend or was he in fact an historical person?," and "If historical, what are we to make of him?"

Beginning with a thumbnail sketch of human history — a summary which economically sweeps through centuries in mere moments of lucid analysis — the author leads gently into a new and vibrant style of presenting Christian evidences which he accomplishes with warmth, wit and integrity. The author draws from our common human experiences and employs compelling logic which makes sense to both the intuitive and the rational thought processes within each of us. He brings us to know the man Jesus as intimately as we might know a life-long friend — up close and personal. The result is a realistic picture of Jesus etched graphically on our consciousness and asking to be considered with openness and candor.

Although clearly the product of careful research, this book is not simply another scholarly review of traditional Christian evidences. Presented conversationally as between two friends, the message of this unique book reaches the heart of the reader because it comes from the heart of an author who confesses to being a fellow struggler in the often elusive search for truth.

The central feature of the book is the insightful approach hinted at in the book's title. Uniquely, the author pits the seemingly unbelievable signs and claims of Jesus against his clearly undeniable character and teaching. The evidences for and against Jesus are presented with a remarkable objectivity which invites the reader to draw his own conclusions about the man Jesus.

Woodroof is one of few Christian authors willing to share honestly and frankly in the skeptical questioning of the secular mind, even if it means admitting seemingly damaging evidence. Even so, his case for an unbelievable yet undeniable Jesus is such a persuasive ordering of the available evidence that, I dare say, few honest readers will be able to withhold a favorable verdict.

F. LaGard Smith
Pepperdine University
Malibu, CA

Preface

This book is written for the skeptic — both religious and non-religious, churched and unchurched — that multitude of men and women whose home is everywhere, whose questions are many and answers are few, whose peace is tenuous and hope is tarnished; whose face is familiar, for doubt is a brother to us all. This book is written for you.

You may be one of the millions a census would identify as a "believer" because you classified yourself as either "Catholic, Protestant or Jew." Yet, though you were born and raised in one of these major religions, you may never have worked through the evidence about the existence of God or the reported claims of Jesus.

In fact, it may never have occurred to you that you should.

Your parents had you inducted into the fold of established religion as an infant, and you were kept there by parental, social and peer pressure. Out of habit you quoted the creed and recited the ritual but never came to grips with whether you believed or not. This book is written for you.

On the other hand, you may be one of the millions a census would identify as an "unbeliever" because you answered the question, "Catholic? Protestant? or Jew?" with a resolute "No!" Long ago you weighed formal religion in the balance and found it wanting. All the injustice and hurt done in the name of religion did not square with your idea of right. The inquisitions, intolerance and iniquity which have at times characterized established religion turned you off years ago.

Or the seeming irrelevance of all the ritual may have created in you feelings similar to those of Moishe Rosen, author of *Jews For Jesus:*

9

My father's belief — "religion is a racket" — made more and more sense to me as I got older. Jewish traditions might be all right, but liturgical rigmarole and irrelevant theology seemed to be all the local synagogue had to offer. I was a practical, hard-working young man, completely unspiritual. Like all good Jewish boys, I felt an intense loyalty to my family. But my ethical approach to the outside world was thoroughly pragmatic: I liked to get along with other people because life was easier that way, but I felt no particular desire to find a divine will for my life.[1]

Or maybe it's the hypocrisy you have seen in established religion that turned you off. There is (and always has been) plenty of hypocrisy in the ranks of the religious.

And you can add other things about established religion that offend you: pomp, power and politics; television evangelists who hawk their wares like side show barkers at a circus. You name it, and it's been done in the name of religion. And you're turned off. This book is for you.

This book is written for all who are open to legitimate evidence regardless of its source or implications. Its goal is to present objectively the evidence about Jesus of Nazareth to the open minds of honest but undecided seekers. Since there is no such thing as total objectivity nor complete honesty, this goal is idealistic. But this shouldn't keep us from trying. Awareness of the ideal and of our failure to achieve it may help erect some safeguards and provide some checks and balances which will aid us in our quest. It will help keep us honest.

This book is designed to serve mainly as a resource to aid those who actually do not know whether or not they believe. It will attempt to arrive at conclusions neither prematurely nor presumptuously. The book attempts to approach the subject at hand as a spelunker (an explorer of underground caves who probes the unknown, regardless of where it may bring him out), not as an engineer (one who knows already where he wants to go and does whatever is necessary to get there).

Your final decision regarding the man from Nazareth is a personal matter, but this book presents some materials which deserve your consideration if you are to render a fair judgment. And a fair judgment is the least required of men and women of intelligence and integrity. As C. S. Lewis affirms:

Honest rejection of Christ, however mistaken, will be forgiven and healed — "whosoever shall speak a word against the Son of Man, it will be forgiven him." But to *evade* the Son of Man; to look the other way; to pretend you haven't noticed; to become suddenly absorbed in something on the other side of the street; to leave the receiver off the telephone because it might be He who was ringing up; to leave unopened certain letters in a strange handwriting because they might be from Him — that is a different matter. You may not be certain yet whether you ought to be a Christian; but you do know you ought to be a man, not an ostrich hiding its head in the sands.[2]

For "if Christianity is untrue, then no honest man will want to believe it, however helpful it might be; if it is true, every honest man will want to believe it, even if it gives him no help at all."[3]

James S. Woodroof

---

1. Moishe Rosen, with William Proctor, *Jews For Jesus* (Old Tappan, New Jersey: Fleming H. Revell Company, 1946), p. 21.

2. C. S. Lewis, "Man or Rabbit?," *God In The Dock* (Grand Rapids: William B. Eerdmans Publishing Co., 1970), p. 111.

3. Ibid.

SECTION I

INTRODUCTION

1

Between A Rock And A Hard Place

He looked more like Rocky Balboa's fight manager than he did a popular Christian apologist. Unkempt, gravel-voiced, bull-doggedly frank, the old man on the BBC intrigued me.

I'm thinking back some eighteen years to the times I watched Malcolm Muggeridge speak his mind on New Zealand television. Still sharp in mind, that aging pugilist would 'tell it like it is' without flinching. All who knew him were aware that he had spent most of his adult life as an avowed atheist. But in the latter rounds he came out fighting for the very thing he had spent his life denying. About the same time I heard him on New Zealand television (1968) Muggeridge made his farewell rectorial address at the University of Edinburgh. The famous satirist and former editor of *Punch* called upon his audience of contemporary students to admit humanism's failure to bring about the utopian society it had so boldly promised: "We all know," he said, "how increasingly hollow and unconvincing it is — the great society, mankind coming of age, men like gods, all the unspeakable cant of Utopians on the run."

Though I wasn't at St. Giles in Edinburgh to hear him make his bold statement, judging from his television presence and the circumstances surrounding his resignation as Rector, I'm sure the gruff old fighter looked his young audience

15

straight in the eye when he said, "As far as I am concerned, it is Christ or nothing." And he told why:

> So I came back to where I began, to the other king, one Jesus, to the Christian notion that man's efforts to make himself personally and collectively happy in earthly terms are doomed to failure. He must, indeed, as Christ said, be born again, be a new man, or he's nothing. So at least I have concluded, having failed to find in past experience, present dilemmas and future expectations, any alternative proposition.[1]

Thus Muggeridge, long-time atheist and proponent of humanism, described his total disillusionment with that course and his adopting the only alternative he considered viable: Jesus Christ.

Others have shared similar experiences. J. B. Phillips, in *Ring of Truth*,[2] recounts the sudden and unexpected reaffirmation of his faith. In that surprising little volume he described the many serendipities he stumbled upon while translating the accounts of Jesus' life. One such discovery he relates:

> What happened to me as the work progressed was that the figure of Jesus emerged more and more clearly, and in a way unexpectedly. Of course I had a deep respect, indeed a great reverence for the conventional Jesus Christ whom the Church worshipped. But I was not at all prepared for the unconventional man revealed in these terse Gospels. No one could have invented such a person: this was no puppet-hero built out of the imaginations of adoring admirers. "This man Jesus" so briefly described, rang true, sometimes alarmingly true. I began to see now why the religious Establishment of those days wanted to get rid of him at all costs. He was sudden death to pride, pomposity and pretense.[3]

Exposure to the gospel records re-affirmed and deepened Phillips' faith.

Phillips also told of a BBC interview with the noted translator Dr. E. V. Rieu:[4] Confessed Dr. Rieu, "My personal reason for doing this [translation of the Gospels] was my own intense desire to satisfy myself as to the authenticity and the spiritual content of the Gospels . . . I approached them in the same spirit as I would have approached them had they been presented to me as recently discovered Greek manuscripts . . ."

Phillips asked Rieu: "Did you get the feeling that the whole thing was alive even while one was translating?"

Rieu replied: "I got the deepest feeling that I possibly could have expected. It . . . changed me; my work changed me. And I came to the conclusion that these words bear the seal of . . . the Son of Man and God. And they are the Magna Carta of the human spirit."

Phillips observed, "They bore to [Dr. Rieu], as to me, the ring of truth."

What, if any, was the common denominator among these scholars which brought them out of either atheism or 'ho-humism' into a vibrant, well-thought-out faith in Jesus? It was their exposure to the record of Jesus' life. At least for them (and they represent some of the best minds and some of the most diverse backgrounds of the 20th century), Jesus was a viable alternative.

I am suggesting the same course of action: an unbiased look at Jesus of Nazareth. Put him to the test. I know of no fairer proposition. I am proposing you accept the material recorded in Matthew, Mark, Luke and John on its own merit, allow it to speak for itself and then draw your own conclusion. Surely, if men who have spent their lives delving into ancient texts of all sorts can justify approaching the Gospels as any other understandable and reliable historical document, the ordinary person can't be too far off base doing the same.

"On its own merit?" you may be thinking. "All the gospel writers were disciples of Jesus. They must have been prejudiced." But as Will Durant, who specialized in analyzing records of antiquity, observed:

> Despite the prejudices and theological preconceptions of the evangelists, they record many incidents that mere inventors would have concealed — the competition of the apostles for high places in the kingdom, their flight after Jesus' arrest, Peter's denial, the failure of Christ to work miracles in Galilee, the references of some auditors to his possible insanity, his early uncertainty as to his mission, his confessions of ignorance as to the future, his moments of bitterness, his despairing cry on the cross; no one reading these scenes can doubt the reality of the figure behind them. That a few simple men in one generation have invented so powerful and appealing a personality, so lofty an ethic, and so inspiring a vision of human brotherhood, would be a miracle far more incredible than any recorded in the Gospels. After two centuries of Higher Criticism the life, character, and teaching of Christ remain reasonably clear, and constitute the most fascinating feature in the history of Western man.[5]

The biblical accounts of Jesus' life *were* recorded by men who were his disciples. But this fact stands in their favor as far as the issue of accuracy is concerned. Those men had been either eyewitnesses themselves or they related the accounts of eyewitnesses of the alleged events and teachings of Jesus. John's gospel, though intimate, linguistically simple and un-professional, is attested by the strongest personal affirmation: "The man who saw it has given testimony, and his testimony is true. He knows that he tells the truth" (19:35). It also possesses a unique, though mystifying, corroboration in the "we" statement of 21:24: "This is the disciple who testifies to these things and who wrote them down. *We* know that his testimony is true" (21:24).

But there is also the professional quality which character-izes the Gospel of Luke. Sir William Ramsay (one of the great-est archaeologists ever to have lived) concluded that Luke was "a historian of the first rank . . . this author should be placed along with the very greatest of historians."[6] Read Luke's introduction and see if you don't agree that it has an authentic, professional ring to it:

> Many have undertaken to draw up an account of the things that have been fulfilled among us, just as they were handed down to us by those who from the first were eyewitnesses and servants of the word. Therefore, since I myself have carefully investigated every-thing from the beginning, it seemed good also to me to write an orderly account for you, most excellent Theophilus, so that you may know the certainty of the things you have been taught. (Lk. 1:1-4).

With that introduction Luke proceeds in 3:1 to establish with pinpoint accuracy[7] the historical setting in which the alleged events took place. Listen to the details:

> In the fifteenth year of the reign of Tiberius Caesar — when Pontius Pilate was governor of Judea, Herod tetrarch of Galilee, his brother Philip tetrarch of Iturea and Trachonitis, and Lysanias tetrarch of Abilene — and during the high-priesthood of Annas and Caiphas . . .

In one sense, though Luke's not being an eyewitness may have prolonged his own coming to faith, it can be an asset to us since this removes him from any emotional attachment he might have possessed had he been a personal acquaintance of Jesus. Not being an eyewitness forced Luke to rely on meticu-lous research for what he recorded (see Luke 1:3). This provided him an opportunity for objectivity which must be considered by any critic an advantage.

There also existed an effective safeguard against unconscious inaccuracy or conscious, deliberate falsehood in that "the New Testament accounts of Christ were being circulated within the lifetimes of those alive at the time of his life. These people could certainly confirm or deny the accuracy of the accounts."[8]

As F. F. Bruce observes:

> . . . it was not only friendly eyewitnesses that the early preachers had to reckon with; there were others less well disposed who were also conversant with the main facts of the ministry and death of Jesus. The disciples could not afford to risk inaccuracies (not to speak of willful manipulation of the facts), which would at once be exposed by those who would be only too glad to do so. On the contrary, one of the strong points in the original apostolic preaching is the confident appeal to the knowledge of the hearers; they not only said, "We are witnesses to these things," but also, "As you yourselves also know" (Acts 2:22). Had there been any tendency to depart from the facts in any material respect, the possible presence of hostile witnesses in the audience would have served as a further corrective."[9]

Though admitting difficulties a liberal theologian might find in the gospel records, Harry Emerson Fosdick acknowledged "the realistic situation confronting Jesus' biographers cannot be successfully fitted into the supposition that they were constructing a myth around an allegorical figure. Our gospels spring from a bona fide historical background. . . ."[10]

And again regarding the gospel records, Fosdick said, "they were composed to meet the needs of widely separated churches, and the marvel is not their differences but their agreement. Seen against the background of the historic situation out of which they came they are authentic endeavors to deal with bona fide recollections of a real personality."[11]

The preceeding material is included not as an effort to prove the claims of the biblical records but simply to establish that the records themselves are legitimate historical documents and a reasonable starting point in our quest. We merely clear some room for ourselves to get on with the investigation. As Elton Trueblood observed, "We require a place to start

which is both concrete and meaningful. Recognizing the falli-
bility of the human mind, we do not expect, as did Descartes,
to find something 'indubitable' to begin with, but we do have a
right to look for something which has reasonable stability."[12]
The sheer magnitude and durability of the Bible's influence
requires that we admit it to have, in Trueblood's terminology,
"reasonable stability."

Also, as we will see in Chapter 2, it is appropriate to separate the Bible from the authoritarian institutions of the past or
present. Thus we risk nothing in granting the story of Jesus,
the central message of the Bible, a hearing. Such an openness
says we are willing to take the documents on their own merit;
to grant them a fair hearing. We are saying, simply, that we
are willing to come to the documents with as few presupposi-
tions of our own as possible. It is an effort to be unbiased; an
attempt to be objective. Honesty requires this much of us.

Honesty also requires us to recognize the kind of evidence
at our disposal in the gospel accounts and treat it with proper
respect — with no more or no less weight than it deserves. The
biblical records consist totally of secondary evidence — the
report of things others have seen, not things we ourselves have
seen. There is a difference . . ., "A very great difference,"
observed D. M. Baillie, "between knowing such a person as the
disciples knew him, and reading about him in a fragmentary
record long afterwards. . . . To live alongside of Jesus in the
flesh was one thing, but to have that episode as simply an
historical memory after Jesus had departed was quite
another."[13]

Any serious study of Jesus must recognize and respect this
change of venue. To say, "I know you believe such and such; it
is in the Bible" is not a legitimate use of the evidence, and I
wonder if it ever was a legitimate use of a written account read
long after an event allegedly occurred. Such an approach to the
gospel records requires one to believe some pretty unbelievable
things simply because biblical writers said they happened. If
faith must be based on blind acceptance of a story told by
people one has never met, I would be among the first to join
the ranks of the skeptical. The validity of Christianity cannot
be established either subjectively ("My feelings tell me . . ."),
institutionally ("The Church teaches . . ."), familially ("My

parents said . . .") or socially ("Everybody believes . . .").
Such parroting of traditional cliches will not stand up under
the current spotlight of investigation.

At the same time, to disqualify automatically the biblical
report simply because it claims things which reside outside the
range of our experience is equally invalid. One must be willing
to give the record regarding Jesus a fair hearing long enough
to determine whether or not its claims are credible.

And so we find ourselves between the proverbial rock and a
hard place, pressed to evaluate at times seemingly contradictory evidence and base our lives on that evaluation. But this
dilemma is a familiar position for the inhabitants of planet
earth. We've been there a thousand times. If we will be true to
the evidence and true to ourselves, we should come out alright.

The remaining chapters present, first, an assessment of our
20th century, western mindset to help us understand how we
got where we are; and, second, a suggested method for pursuing and processing the available evidence about Jesus of
Nazareth as a possible alternative.

1. Malcolm Muggeridge, "Another King," *Jesus Rediscovered* (New York: Doubleday & Company, Inc., 1969), p. 58.

2. J. B. Phillips, *Ring of Truth* (London: Hodder And Staughton, 1967).

3. Ibid., p. 64.

4. Ibid., pp. 55, 56.

5. Will Durant, *Caesar and Christ,* in *The Story of Civilization,* vol. 3 (New York: Simon and Schuster, 1944), p. 557.

6. Sir William Ramsey, *The Bearing of Recent Discovery on the Trustworthiness of the New Testament* (London: Hodder and Stoughton, 1915), p. 222.

7. Daniel-Rops, Op. cit., p. 12ff.

8. Josh McDowell, *More Than A Carpenter* (Wheaton, Ill.: Living Books, 1985), p. 51.

9. F. F. Bruce, *The New Testament Documents: Are They Reliable?* (Downers Grove, Ill.: Intervarsity Press, 1964), pp. 16, 33.

10. Harry Emerson Fosdick, *The Man From Nazareth* (New York: Harper & Brothers, 1949), p. 38.

11. Ibid., p. 40.

12. Elton Trueblood, *A Place to Stand* (New York: Harper & Row, 1969), p. 38.

13. D. M. Baillie, *Faith In God* (London: Faber and Faber, n.d.), p. 261.

2

How Did We Get There?

(A Spelunker's Guide To Western Thought)

In case you are the impatient type who likes to barge right into the unknown without pausing at the mouth of the cavern to check your map and determine your location, you might prefer to skip this chapter and go immediately to Chapter 3. But if you believe it's safer first to see where you are in relation to what you are exploring, you'll want to read this chapter in order to get your bearings.

Checking our map, then, we locate the *"You Are Here"* marker and discover that where we are is a long way from where we were! "Something has happened to contemporary Western man. He is not thinking as he did thirty or forty years ago."[1] Gerard Phillips says modern man "has not simply acquired a new way of feeling, thinking and living; he has literally become someone else, and he scarcely recognizes himself. . . ."[2] Who is this "someone else" contemporary Western man has become? And how did he come to be? This chapter will attempt to answer these two questions.

Historically and traditionally, Western man has been considered by virtually all observers to be essentially Judeo-Christian. He was considered so because of two basic premises he had held for many centuries: 1) *God is* and 2) *the Bible is God's Book.* Life in the West was shaped by these two premises. The legal system, moral code, and customs; the idioms, the literature, music and art; the social institutions and work ethic — all were rooted in biblical soil.[3] Werner Keller in his book, *The Bible As History,* points up this obvious fact: "No book in the whole history of mankind has had such a revolutionary influence, has so decisively affected the development of the western world . . . as the Bible."[4]

But no longer can it be assumed that Western man believes in God or accepts the Bible as God's word. This dramatic shift has affected every facet of the Western mind-set. It has altered man's concept of himself, of God and of others. It has challenged every value once held dear and every foundation once considered essential to civilization. The West's orientation has shifted.

Exactly when this change took place is difficult to ascertain because of the subtlety of the shift and the enormous philosophical distance covered by it. Elton Trueblood, in his book, *The Predicament of Man,* identifies the turning point as World War II.[5] Gerard Phillips agrees.[6] Francis Schaeffer, in his book, *The God Who Is There,* pushes back the turning point to World War I.[7] Paul Tillich put the emergence of this new, re-oriented man at mid-nineteenth century.[8] All of these analysts were attempting to identify the time at which the tip of the iceberg began noticeably to rip through the hull of Western man's thinking. The extent of the damage became more visible about the time cited by Trueblood and Schaeffer.

At that approximate time the Western psyche suffered a double blow. Not only had biblical authority eroded significantly, but humanism (the philosophy that man, not God, is the center of the universe) was also being discredited.[9] Humanism's optimistic claim for humankind that "things are getting better and better."[10] was seriously undermined by the utter cruelty and inhumanity of two world wars. The general effect of this double blow is that Western man has been left like a ship without a rudder and listing badly.

The West has little, if any, unified philosophy. An encroaching wave of pluralism threatens to engulf mankind. Western man doesn't quite know where he is. The euphoria which at first had accompanied the advent of humanism turned first to confusion and then to despair. In the words of

Landon Saunders, national radio speaker, Western man began to sense he was "alone . . . in a closed system . . . alienated and estranged from anything that is like he is other than himself which he distrusts at this point. He has no absolute Source from which to draw meaning for his existence. He is a giant question mark."[11]

Paul Tillich, whose existential theology contributed to the present condition, observed that "since the middle of the nineteenth century, a movement has arisen in the Western world which expresses the anxiety about the meaning of our existence, including the problems of death, faith, and guilt. In our present day literature, many names are given to this phenomenon . . . Wasteland . . . No Exit . . . Age of Anxiety . . . Neurotic Character of Our Times . . . Man Against Himself . . . Encounter With Nothingness. . . ."[12]

Though the shift became visible at the beginning of the twentieth century, its seeds were sown hundreds of years earlier through a dramatic change in the way man thought — in man's approach to knowledge. The means by which we know what we know underwent a drastic transformation.[13] This Renaissance (or rebirth), as the new age came to be called, swept first over Europe and then westward with unequaled force and eventually replaced God with man as the center of the universe. It is in this precarious position that Western civilization finds itself aground in the final years of the 20th Century.

Let's go back and trace briefly from the beginning the process that has brought us to where we are today. We will look at the process in outline only — a "thumbnail sketch" — since the object of this book is not to discern how we got into the present state but to present evidence for pursuing an alternate course. To help us establish some parameters for our thinking it will be helpful to call attention to five basic eras involved in the shift. They are: 1) The Era of Authority, 2) The Era of Authoritarianism, 3) The Era of Humanitarianism, 4) The Era of Humanism and 5) The Era of Secularism. Notice first:

THE ERA OF AUTHORITY

Authority is a social ordering *without which man cannot live.* For thousands of years man has depended on certain authoritative standards (civil, social, religious) to determine right and wrong, good and evil, truth and error. Human beings cannot live in close proximity to other human beings without there existing some mutually accepted standard of conduct. For confirmation of this, one needs no further evidence than the massive traffic jams which occur when traffic signals break down, or the shameful toll of human lives taken by international terrorists who violate standards of international conduct. Peaceful co-existence demands mutually accepted standards of authority.

For Western man the unifying standard of authority has been the moral law of the Jewish nation, refined and exemplified in the life and teachings of Jesus of Nazareth, and generally known as the Judeo-Christian Ethic. It has been the foremost determining factor in the development of the customs and mores, the constants and morality, the social conscience and sense of "ought" which characterize Western man. The influence of the Judeo-Christian moral force on the Western mind has been so pervasive as to make it highly unlikely that anyone born into Western culture and nourished by its traditions could think independently of that code of ethics.

The Judeo-Christian ethic is contained essentially in the Ten Commandments (recorded in Ex. 20:1-17).

1. I am the Lord your God . . . You shall have no other gods before me.
2. You shall make for yourself no graven image.
3. You shall not take the name of the Lord your God in vain.
4. Remember the sabbath day to keep it holy.
5. Honor your father and your mother.
6. You shall not murder.
7. You shall not commit adultery.
8. You shall not steal.
9. You shall not bear false witnesses.
10. You shall not covet.

The first major influence of this period was Moses (ca. 1500-1380 B.C.), the distinguished lawgiver who led the Israelites from Egyptian slavery into the land of Canaan, and whose name this code bears. The Jewish prophets, most of whom lived and wrote during the eighth and seventh centuries B.C., were also influential during this period. The Greek philosophers Socrates, Plato and Aristotle, who lived during the 5th and 4th centuries B.C., would not have their greatest influence, even upon the non-Christian world, until over a thousand years later.

The second major influence in the era of authority was Jesus of Nazareth (4 B.C.-29 A.D.). According to Christian scriptures, Moses wrote of Jesus when he said, "The Lord your God will raise up for you a prophet like me from among your own people; you must listen to everything he tells you. Anyone who does not listen to him will be completely cut off from among his people."[14] Fourteen centuries after Moses' statement Jesus of Nazareth called the Jewish nation to a clearer understanding of, and a rededication to, the heart and soul of the Law of Moses, saying:

"Love the Lord your God with all your heart, and with all your soul and with all your mind." This is the first and greatest commandment. And the second is like it: "Love your neighbor as yourself." All the Law and the Prophets hang on these two commandments. (Matt. 22:37-40).

The practical application of this monumental moral axiom lay dormant during the centuries prior to Jesus. But with his coming, the high ethical standards expressed in the Decalogue, combined with the dynamic of Jesus' own life, elevated and spread that moral and ethical code to virtually all Western nations. Thus the Western world adopted an authority by which to live. With only the briefest introspection, any Westerner can see how broad, if not deep, has been the influence of the Judeo-Christian ethic on his life.

Paul (ca. 1 - 65 A.D.), a disciple of Jesus, is the third major influence. A Jewish scholar and activist around the beginning of the Christian era, Paul dramatically converted from Judaism to Christianity.[15] He traveled, preached extensively and wrote at least thirteen documents with authority he claimed was given him by the resurrected Christ. He was martyred about 65 A.D. Next to Jesus, Paul was the most influential personality in the spread of Christianity.

In addition to Paul, there were in the early years of Christianity men of lesser influence such as Peter, John, James, Matthew, Mark and Luke. Though Peter exerted a significant influence during the beginning years of the Christian movement, his contribution to the authority of the period was not as significant initially as it was much later when his name was heavily relied upon by the Roman church to secure the papacy's claim of authority.

Overall, the *Era of Authority* lasted from 1400 B.C. (the approximate date of the Decalogue) to 313 A.D. (the year the Christian religion was legalized in the Roman Empire by the Imperial Edict of Milan), at which time a second era was ushered onto the scene:

THE ERA OF AUTHORITARIANISM

With the conversion of Constantine and the legalization of Christianity, a subtle change began to take place regarding the nature of authority. Generally speaking, there began a transition from authority under God to authoritarianism under Roman ecclesiastical rule.

This transition began with the conversion of Constantine (306 A.D.). Christian tradition has it that, on the night before Constantine attacked Maxentius and the Roman army, he had a dream in which he saw a sign accompanied by the words: "Hoc signo victor eris!" ("By this sign you shall be the victor.") The sign consisted of a cross and the Greek letters Chi-Rho, the first two letters of the name Christ. Constantine construed this to indicate Christ's support of his cause. Bolstered by this perceived affirmation he won the battle the next day and, consequently, became Emperor of Rome and imperial mentor of the Roman church. But it is now generally accepted that many of the developments which began with the conversion of Constantine did not prove to be true to the main thrust of the Christian gospel.

After the conversion of Constantine human freedom increasingly was overridden by autocratic and unChristian ecclesiastical institutions.[16] The church's confrontation with the heathen nations more nearly resembled conquest than conversion. The campaigns of the church became synonymous with the conquests of Rome. In this way, the Roman church spread wherever the power of Imperial Rome spread. Thus all of Europe came under the sway of the authority of Rome, both secular and spiritual.

By the time of the fall of Western Imperial Rome (ca. 476 A.D.), the presence and power of the Roman church was already in place, filling the void left by the demise of Western Imperial Rome. Increasingly the supremacy of the Roman pontiff and his absolute authority to rule the universal church was stridently affirmed by Rome and rarely questioned by others. This trend toward a centralized authority had begun with Constantine's restructuring of the church along the lines of the authoritarian government of Rome, but eventually it spilled over into the secular scene as well, with Pope Boniface III claiming authority over all secular rulers. Thus Constantine had paved the way for the absolute rule of the papacy which reached its peak during the reign of Pope Gregory in 1075.

Papal power waxed and waned during the years that followed. With the reign of Pope Boniface VIII (1294-1303) it became obvious that, though the papacy claimed complete power, in reality it no longer possessed it. Thus the general period of *Authoritarianism* is identified as 313 A.D. to 1300 A.D. By the beginning of the 14th century, it was evident that ecclesiastical authoritarianism was a system *under which man would not live.* The winds of change eventually toppled the authoritarian rule of the medieval church.

Before leaving this period we should identify a condition in the medieval church which, more than any other factor, contributed to the ushering in of the new age. It was a *spiritual* secularism which Roman Catholicism and other "official" churches created in their own communicants. The following practices and conditions of the medieval church are here identified as having wove the fabric of the new age; the result being that, long before secularism reduced modern man to a non-entity, the authoritarian religions of the day had already accomplished it, or at least had set the stage for it. If, as Peter Gay suggests, the Classical Age of Greece was the signpost to secularism,[17] medieval ecclesiasticism was the road which led to it. If the Classical Age was the womb for secularism, the medieval church was the midwife who delivered it. The contributing factors were these:

1) The Christening of Infants, a basic practice of the major medieval churches, shifted the responsibility of faith from the individual to the family, immediate and extended, thus diminishing the importance of the individual communicant.

2) The Sacerdotal (priestly) System, which lay at the heart of the medieval church, inserted a priest between the communicant and God in two ways which diminished the importance of the individual: In the Mass the communicant became a spectator of someone else's action, and in the Confessional the communicant became dependent on someone else's intercession.[18]

3) The Prayer System, which imposed a host of saints between the communicant and God, diminished still further the place of the individual.

4) The Latin Mass, retained for hundreds of years after Latin had ceased to be the language of the common people, was an intellectual put-down which further reduced the importance of the individual.

5) The Total Authority of the Church robbed medieval man of his right to think and make responsible decisions on his own.

6) Elaborate Ritualism — bordering on superstition and magic — came increasingly to be viewed by thinking people as unrealistic.

7) The Pomp and Opulence of the church in the midst of the poverty and ignorance of the people widened the gap between the institution and the individual.

8) Heavy Reliance Upon Tradition hallowed the past out of proportion to the importance of the present.

9) The Establishment of an official religion of the State (whether Catholic or Protestant), into which infants were initiated without their consent and without legal alternative, set the prevailing conditions in concrete.

As a result of these innovations, the religious institution became the center of reference, and the individual was robbed of his personal identity and worth. From his background in the Danish Lutheran church, Soren Kierkegaard testifies as late as the 19th century to the presence of this secularization of religion. He writes about the case of a man who doubts that he is a Christian:

> If he happened to be married, his wife would say to him: "Dear husband of mine, how can you get such notions into your head? How can you doubt that you are a Christian? Are you not a Dane, and does not geography say that the Lutheran form of the Christian religion is the ruling religion in Denmark? For you are surely not a Jew, nor are you a Mohammedan; what then can you be if not a Christian? It is a thousand years since paganism was driven out of Denmark, so I know you are not a pagan. Do you not perform your duties at the office like a conscientious civil servant; are you not a good citizen of a Christian nation, a Lutheran Christian state? So then of course you must be a Christian."[19]

Having thus been robbed of his personal identity by the prevailing religious systems, medieval man walked with mounting excitement into the arms of the oncoming humanist revolution.

THE ERA OF HUMANITARIANISM

This period, best described as an awakening, a release from the shackles of ignorance and a restoring of the dignity of mankind, was a state *in which man longed to live.* Unfortunately, in comparison to the many centuries humanism has held sway in the thinking of modern man, the era of humanitarianism was very brief.[20] The period of humanism is usually dated from Desiderius Erasmus (1466?-1536), the "prince of the humanists."[21] But the humanism of Erasmus was quite different from that which emerged a mere seventy-five years afterwards. Erasmus' humanism possessed the naivete and simplicity that often characterize fledgling movements. It more nearly resembled humanitarianism than it did modern-day humanism.[22]

The all-too-brief period of humanitarianism was an exciting time. The movement spread over Europe like a breath of fresh air, reviving literature and the arts and causing an upsurge in science and commerce. Ralph L. Lewis describes the emergence of the new Renaissance man:

A multitude of mariners plied the seven seas, circled the globe, claimed new continents. Self surfaced; the individual, freedom, personal worth and independence rose to highest values. Tradition and bondage to the past lost their grip. Authority weakened. Experience, exploration and experimentation thrived as prime movers in the human arena. . . . The individual surfaced; the institution was no longer the only hand on the helm. The people began to be involved.[23]

But as a stream is purer at its head waters than it is at its mouth, so was the humanism of Erasmus than that which followed. In this regard Matthew Spinka expresses regret that "the humanist movement, which was and could continue to be of tremendous benefit to the cause of Christianity, henceforth diverged ever more markedly into a development essentially contrary and inimical to the Christian world view. Zwingli and Calvin were markedly humanistic although they utilized classical learning for the benefit of their vigorous Christian convictions. But such was not the case with other outstanding representatives of humanism, who turned the movement into channels eventuating in the complete secularism and irreligious scientism of our own day."[24]

THE ERA OF HUMANISM

Humanism is a philosophy *which eventually robbed man of the ultimate reason to live*. In the new humanist orientation, man, not God, became the measure of all things. "Modern man . . . increasingly emancipated himself from all tutelage of the Church — in fact, from all relation to the spiritual . . . all genuine interest in the spiritual implications of human life was ultimately largely abandoned. . . ."[25]

The irretrievable tragedy of the transition into the new age was that the authority of the Bible was equated with the increasingly absolute, and often oppressive, authoritarianism of the Roman Church and its rival counterparts: the Anglican and the Russian and Greek Orthodox churches. It was assumed, almost without a second thought, that to throw off the one was, automatically, to throw off the other. God himself was dethroned at the same time authoritarian, institutionalized religion was disavowed. Man took center stage. As Francis Schaeffer observed: "Renaissance humanism steadily evolved toward modern humanism — a value system rooted in the belief that man is his own measure, that man is autonomous, totally independent."[26] But in declaring this to be its direction, humanism set itself on a collision course with self-destruction. It would lead eventually to the dehumanizing of humanity and drive humanism to the precipice of nihilism, the philosophy that all existing moral, religious, social, political and economic institutions must be completely destroyed.[27]

Malcolm Muggeridge, in his *Chronicles of Wasted Time*, describes in haunting language the years he spent advocating humanism. Of the "monstrous Niagara of words" which flowed from his pen during those years he laments:

> I confess they signify to me a lost life. Possibilities vaguely envisaged but never realized. A light glimpsed, only to disappear. Something vaguely caught, as it might be distant music or an elusive fragrance; something full of enchantment and the promise of ecstasy. Far, far away, and yet near; at the very farthermost rim of time and space, and in the palm of my hand. In any case, whether strained after in the remote distance, or reached for near at hand — unattained. No light seen more enduring than a match flickering out in a dark cave. No lasting ecstasy experienced, only a door closed, and footsteps echoing ever more faintly down stone stairs.[28]

There were many philosophers and theologians who played a part in this process,[29] but the utter decay of humanism became most evident in the works of Ludwig Feuerbach (1804-1872), an exponent of humanistic atheism, and Karl Marx (1818-1883), father of Communism. With the nihilism of Friedrich Nietzsche (1844-1900) and his Superman ethic we see humanism pushed to its logical conclusion. As Spinka observed:

> Thus the age [of humanism] has turned upon itself in repudiating its own past. The distinguishing characteristic of that past is that it made man the measure of all things. Now man has ceased to be the highest value: his place is taken by technics. Marx has subordinated him to the well-being of society and thus deprived him of his spiritual nature. Man has become a tender of machines. Nietzsche went even further: he not only proclaimed that "God is dead," for by denying God he inevitably denied the spiritual worth of man as well; and he followed his own logic by advocating the extermination of the "herdman" in favor of an imagined, non-existent "Superman."[30]

But Nietzsche could not bear the implications of his own theory. Having moved to Switzerland in 1881 where he did much of his work until 1888, he became mentally incapacitated — either through disease or the natural consequences of his own extreme philosophy.[31] Thus, in the words of Muggeridge, humanism had brought "no lasting ecstasy . . ., only a door closed, and footsteps echoing ever more faintly down stone stairs" to the final stage of humanism:

THE ERA OF SECULARISM

Secularism — humanism in its extreme — is the era *in which man sees no reason to allow others to live* except as objects of his own self-interests. We are presently living in the era of Secularism. Spinka observed: "The new age dawned, as far as physical science and techniques are concerned, early in the present century, when Einstein discovered the tremendous energy locked in the atom."[32] That event, however, was only the above-ground explosion which hurled modern man irretrievably into the Secularistic/Scientistic Age; because, as Schubert M. Ogden observed, "ever since the seventeenth century, science and technology have been effecting . . . a radical transformation in our understanding of ourselves and our environment. . . ."[33] Ogden predicted: "The scientific world picture is here to stay and will assert its rights against any theology, however imposing, that conflicts with it. So far as his knowledge of the world is concerned, modern man long ago opted for the method of science and therewith decided irrevocably for secularity."[34]

Scientism affirms that "the general scientific method is not only the sole means for obtaining knowledge about the world disclosed by our senses, but this kind of knowledge is the only kind of knowledge there is."[35] Consequently, "Something of a new . . . cult developed in the popular mind, which reflected how popular opinion had switched its allegiance from Christian orthodoxy to science and technology. The preface 'The church teaches . . .' and 'The Bible says . . .' came to be replaced by 'Science teaches . . .,'" 'The scientists have shown that . . .' "[36]

Spinka called this age "Scientism" and defined it as the view that "science does now or will in time provide a complete and final answer to all human problems — as a substitute for both the religious and humanistic world views."[37] Accordingly, "the predominant mood among the majority of secularists is not so much a formulated conviction as an almost unconscious lack of interest in, and an utter indifference to, all religious concerns. As a rule they aim solely at the goal of physical well-being, a high standard of living."[38]

This sounds all too familiar as we look both inward and around us at the general Western value system which we see so much in evidence. According to one survey,[39] Western man believes:

* Everything is relative;
* What can't be proved can't be believed;
* Scientific knowledge is certain and the standard of truth; Matters of faith are uncertain;
* Beyond death nobody knows;
* "Real" means seen and handled;
* The big things are the great things and, because man is so small in this big universe, he is unimportant;
* I cannot help being what I am;
* Freedom means doing what I like;
* Justice means equality;
* To put religion first is religious arrogance;
* Laws of nature determine everything.

On December 4, 1977, Los Angeles reporter James J. Doyle asked philosopher-historian Will Durant, "Where are we now?" Durant, author of *The Story of Civilization* and recipient of the Pulitzer Prize, answered,

> We're in the stage in which Greece was when the gods ceased to be gods and became mere poetry, and therefore exercised no element of order or command upon human behavior. There was the development of city life, of science and philosophy and the result was a period of pagan license . . . in which morals floundered in an ocean of competing religions. . . . By the time of Caesar you had a permissive society and a pagan society in the sense of sexual enjoyment with minimal moral restraint. Now whether we shall have to wait for a new religion, the way the Greeks and Romans did, because . . . what happened was the old civilization decayed to the point where it cried out for a new religion, for something to worship and obey.[40]

Whereas Durant answered the question, "Where are we now?," the present chapter has attempted to show *why* we are where we are. Hopefully the preceeding material has not only tracked the course but traced the causes that have led us to our present state. We now should be better equipped to pursue the question: "Does modern man have any alternatives?"

1. Landon Saunders, *Working Paper*, unpublished, p. 45.

2. Gerard Phillips, *The Church in the Modern World*, pp. 12, 13, as quoted by James J. Kavanaugh, *Struggle of the Unbeliever* (New York: Trident Press, 1967), p. 117.

3. Daniel-Rops, *Jesus and His Times*, vol. I (Garden City, N.Y.: Image Books, 1958), pp. 36, 37.

4. Werner Keller, *The Bible as History* (London: Hodder and Stoughton, 1956), p. x.

5. D. Elton Trueblood, *The Predicament of Modern Man* (New York: Harper Brothers, 1944), Chapter 1.

6. Phillips, Op. cit., p. 117.

7. Frances Schaeffer, *The God Who Is There* (Downers Grove, Ill.: University Press, 1968), p. 13.

8. Paul Tillich, *Theology of Culture* (New York: Oxford University Press, 1964), p. 207.

9. Os Guinness, *The Dust of Death* (London: InterVarsity Press, 1973), p. 3.

10. The story is told of a French humanist who in his lectures would have his audience repeat the saying, "Every day and in every way I am getting better and better." D. Elton Trueblood, in his book *The Predicament of Modern Man* (Op. cit., pp. 5, 6) cites the optimistic claim of F. S. Marvin which was popular in the 1920s: "And now, of all consolidators, science is showing its supreme fitness and its kinship with the sense of a common humanity. . . . Side by side with the growth of science, which is also the basis of the material prosperity and unification of the world, has come a steady deepening of human sympathy, and the extension of it to all weak and suffering things. . . . Science, founding a firmer basis for the co-operation of mankind, goes widening down the centuries, and sympathy and pity bind the courses together." Trueblood observed, "This hope, by no means rare, is now seen to be utterly unjustified."

11. Saunders, Op. cit., p. 48.

12. Tillich, Op. Cit., p. 207.

13. For a popular treatment of this process see Francis Schaeffer, *The God Who Is There* (Downers Grove, Ill.: InterVarsity Press, 1968).

14. Acts 3:23 quoting Deut. 18:15, 18, 19.

15. See *Acts of Apostles* in the New Testament for the record of Paul's conversion.

16. See Adolph Harnack, *What Is Christianity?* (New York: Harper Brothers, 1957), pp. 210-214. In this lecture (No. 12) Harnack suggests, however, that restriction of freedom was a reality prior to Constantine. The growth of ecclesiasticism magnified it.

17. Peter Gay, *The Enlightenment, An Interpretation* (New York: Vintage Books/Random House, 1968), pp. 72-94.

18. For a look at a companion doctrine (Indulgences) and a modern proliferation of it, see "Christmas Gift," *Time,* Dec. 30, 1985, p. 71, col. 3.

19. S. Kierkegaard, *Concluding Unscientific Postscript,* David F. Swenson and Walter Lowrie, trs. (Princeton: Princeton University Press, 1944), p. 49.

20. As defined in this work, humanism is "humanitarianism stripped of God-consciousness."

21. Matthew Spinka, *Christian Thought From Erasmus to Berdyaev* (Printice-Hall, Inc., Englewood Cliffs, N.J., 1962), p. 14.

22. Guinness, Op. cit., p. 5. Humanitarianism may be distinguished from humanism in the sense that in humanitarianism humans are important, while in humanism they are all-important — to the exclusion of any power or intelligence beyond the human level.

23. Ralph L. and Gregg Lewis, *Inductive Preaching* (Westchester, Ill., Crossway Books, 1983), p. 50.

24. Spinka, op. cit., p. 16.

25. Ibid., p. 6.

26. Francis A. Schaeffer, *How Should We Then Live?* (Crossway Books, Westchester, Ill., 1976), p. 60.

27. "Nihilism," *Webster's New World Dictionary,* 1969.

28. Malcolm Muggeridge, *Chronicles of Wasted Time,* Vol. I, "The Green Stick" (New York: William Morrow & Co., 1973), p. 14.

29. Matthew Spinka in *Christian Thought From Erasmus to Berdyaev* provides a thorough study of this subject. Briefly, at the beginning of the 17th century stand the influential Rene Descartes (1596-1650) and his contemporary Baruch Spinoza (1632-1677). A little later John Locke (1632-1704) and David Hume (1685-1783) emphasized experience and affirmed that empirical evidence was the only basis for knowledge. With a definite Christian bias, Blaise Pascal (1623-1662), Bishop Joseph Butler (1692-1752) and John Wesley (1703-1791) reflect the influence of humanism in the areas of existentialism, rationalism and evangelicalism, respectively.

Among others, Jean-Jacques Rousseau (1712-1778) and F. D. E. Schleirmacher (1768-1834) turned away from rationalism and introduced the age of

Romanticism. Immanuel Kant (1724-1804), the Ethical Imperativist, contributed greatly to the shift toward humanism, as did Friedrich Hegel (1770-1831). French philosopher Auguste Comte (1798-1857) made his contribution as an exponent of positivism. Reacting against the monism of Hegel, Soren Kierkegaard (1813-1855) developed his existentialism and Albrecht Ritschl (1822-1889) his social gospel.

30. Ibid., p. 2.

31. Schaeffer, Op. cit., p. 180.

32. Ibid., p. 1.

33. Schubert M. Ogden, *The Reality of God* (New York: Harper & Row, 1963), p. 7.

34. Ibid., p. 8.

35. Ibid.

36. Lloyd Geering, *God In The New World* (Great Britain, Hodder and Stoughton, 1968), p. 23.

37. Spinka, Op. cit., p. 13.

38. Ibid., p. 3.

39. World Council of Churches, *Man's Disorder and God's Design,* vol. 2: *The Church's Witness To God's Design,* The Amsterdam Assembly Series (New York: Harper and Brothers, 1948), pp. 81, 82.

40. James J. Doyle, "Writing Couple Believes World in Decline Peril," *Memphis Commercial Appeal,* Dec. 4, 1977, Section C, p. 6.

3

Is There A Way Out?

Muggeridge's assessment of the failure of humanism/ secularism: ". . . how increasingly hollow and unconvincing it is," and how his pursuit of humanism had brought "no lasting ecstasy . . . only a door closed, and footsteps echoing ever more faintly down stone stairs" is startling, saddening and sobering: startling in that a man of his age and position found the strength of conviction and the humility of heart to admit the failure of the philosophy which he had passionately pursued and publicly promoted most of his life; saddening in that the vast majority of this planet's population is rushing headlong down the same hollow corridor; sobering in that each of us has been subtly but unquestionably affected by the very humanism Muggeridge renounced, and to the degree we have pursued it we have suffered the same consequences: increasing emptiness and feelings of futility and loneliness; "footsteps echoing ever more faintly down stone stairs."

"But what alternative do I have?" you may be asking. "I know the alternative Muggeridge accepted: Jesus Christ. But his processing the evidence and arriving at that conclusion is not adequate for me. I must find that answer for myself. And here I sit, 2,000 years from Jesus. All I have are historical documents . . . records of his life written by others. Really, what are my chances of knowing the truth about him so I can make a decision — one way or the other?"

Well said! Your questions are appropriate. There are no eyewitnesses today to a life lived 2,000 years ago. No one today possesses primary evidence. The only evidence available is secondary — that which others record *they* saw and heard of Jesus. Is there a legitimate method of examining that kind of evidence with reasonable expectation of resolution?

I believe there is. I will attempt to substantiate this affirmation in the following manner: First, I will state a basic principle involved. Next I will illustrate the principle historically and physically. Having thus examined the principle, I will devote the remainder of the book to a practical application of the principle to our investigation of the identity of Jesus. I think you will be encouraged as you discover also that the method under consideration was the very method Jesus used exclusively to establish his identity. So, it would appear we are on the right track. Let's pick up our gear and be on our way.

The basic principle was barely introduced in Chapter 1, *i.e.,* secondary evidence possesses a different dynamic than primary evidence and must be treated accordingly. Whereas primary evidence (what we have seen with our own eyes, handled, smelled, tasted, etc.) has a tendency to move one to believe, secondary evidence (that which someone tells you they saw, handled, smelled, tasted, etc.) has a tendency to push one to doubt. This is especially true if the thing attested to resides not only outside the realm of our own personal experience but also outside any documented experience of the human race in general. If we have not seen it with our own eyes or if it is not generally attested to as a common human experience, we become skeptical.

And for good reason: the event attested to may not be real. Take, for example, the testimony of an alcoholic suffering from delirium tremens. Vivid and detailed though his visions may be, they are recognized by sober people as having no substance outside the alcoholic's mind. So also is the testimony of the mentally ill who hear voices and see strange sights. When mentally well-balanced people examine such evidence they come to the conclusion the events attested to are not real, but imaginary.

But even when the event is real, secondary evidence attesting to it still requires the hearers to "put two and two together" and draw a conclusion. And even then the outcome is not guaranteed. The same valid evidence may produce faith in some people and doubt in others. Various factors contribute to the conflicting conclusions drawn from the same valid evidence; factors involving the degree of objectivity versus the degree of subjectivity a person may bring to a given problem. Due to the presence or absence of vested interests, biases and blind spots, some people are open to any conclusion to which the evidence might lead, while others are not. According to our familiar figure: some people have a spelunker mindset; some do not.

History is replete with examples of this, but surely one of the clearest is found in the experiences of Heinrich and Sophia Schliemann, discoverers of the ancient city of Troy.[1] In the words of Irving Stone, "The adventures of Henry and Sophia are among the most dramatic that ever happened to two human beings."[2]

Schliemann (1822-1890), who by the age of 44 had made three fortunes — two in Russia and one in California, determined to give the rest of his life to unearthing the ancient city of Troy; Homer's Troy — the Troy scholars of the world said did not exist. Schliemann's friend, Bishop Vimpos, voiced the skepticism of the academic community: "You keep referring to Troy. But there is no Troy! It is a figment of the poet's imagination. Nor was there a Trojan War, or a wooden horse . . . it's all mythology!"[3]

But Schliemann, having been intrigued by Homer's *Iliad* and *Odyssey* from early childhood, believed differently. He knew precisely where Troy was because Homer in the Illiad had told him where it was. And Schliemann was willing to invest a fortune in money and years of his life to prove that conviction. Though Schliemann was accused of being a mere treasure hunter, his personal correspondence (including 750 personal letters and twenty-four vital documents discovered in 1965 in a basement in Athens) corrects that misunderstanding. Biographers Lynn and Gray Pool, who had access to those documents, concluded: "The letters disclose irrefutably that

Schliemann's real goal was not gold or glory, but to separate truth from legend."[4]

But in the minds of most, truth did not separate easily from legend. Even Schliemann's wife to be, the seventeen year old Sophia, was skeptical at first. As she listened on their first meeting to his enthusiastic claims about Troy she was thrown into a dilemma: "He simply can't be a lunatic. He has traveled the world, published two books, made fortunes from his own endeavors. He is egocentric, to be sure, but I doubt that he would expose himself to ridicule."[5]

Others were not so kind, and not without ample cause from Schliemann himself.[6] Schliemann, despite his tremendous discoveries, was called every ugly word in the eighteen languages he spoke and wrote: imposter, thief, fraud, idiot, troublemaker, wastrel.[7] Georgis Nikolaides, a member of the Archaeological Society and author of *The Iliad and Its Topography*, scathingly castigated Schliemann publicly saying that "not one word that Dr. Schliemann was publishing in the *Newspaper of the Debates*, the *Levant Herald* or the periodical of the *Greek Philological Society* had the remotest connection with provable fact. All honest and sensible men knew that Troy could never be found by excavating earth and debris because the city had been created from the whole cloth of Homer's poetic imagination. It existed nowhere except in the pages of the *Iliad*."[8]

But having checked meticulously Homer's references to Troy, in the autumn of 1872 Schliemann began excavating with a passion. He employed hundreds of workers to move thousands of tons of earth at a personal expense of $50,000 in 1872 alone. Finally, after months of digging and with no encouragement or help from the archaeological community, Schliemann struck pay dirt. As the workers unearthed a massive double wall like the one Homer had described in the *Iliad*, Sophia began to tremble with excitement.

"Henry, have you really done it? Have we found the wall built by Poseidon and Apollo?"

"There can be no question about it," replied Henry.

They stood transfixed. Only the sound of the shovels and the thud of the earth into the wheelbarrows broke into the silence.

"Congratulations," Sophia finally whispered. "You were right and the rest of the world was wrong."[9]

On May 31, 1873, the Schliemanns[10] uncovered the priceless "treasure of King Priam" consisting of eight thousand gold and silver artifacts. They hid this incredible treasure and on June 13, 1873, shipped it out of the country aboard the sailing vessel Omonoia. When the shipment arrived in Athens Schliemann secretly stored it in rented quarters and began the laborious task of photographing the entire collection. Having completed this, Schliemann publicized his discovery. Even then, because of their vested interests, and perhaps also because of Schliemann's questionable qualifications and character, many in the academic community did not believe the amateur had discovered Troy. But the common people of Greece did. Schliemann later was recognized by archaeologists in general as having established an historical background for the writings of Homer. "Schliemann's work led to continuing investigations that are revealing in ever-widening horizons the wonders of preclassical Greece (6000 to 1000 B.C.). Before Schliemann this civilization was not even known to have existed."[11]

Just over two years after Schliemann's death, his assistant and successor Wilhelm Dorpfeld completed Schliemann's work and wrote this well-deserved post-mortem on Schliemann's monumental accomplishment at Troy: "The long dispute over the existence of Troy and over its site is at an end. The Trojans have triumphed . . . Schliemann has been vindicated . . . the countless books which in both ancient and modern times have been published against Troy have become meaningless."[12]

Consider momentarily those observers who believed Schliemann. How did they view the evidence so that in the end they came away convinced of its validity? Basically, whether knowingly or unknowingly, they accepted the evidence as "self-corroborative" or "self-substantiative." They were caught between what they could not easily believe (i.e., the historicity of Homer and Troy) and what they could not reasonably deny (i.e., the excavation site and the artifacts), and, based on the quality and quantity of the evidence, they believed.

Let me illustrate physically the dynamic of such evidence. The most primitive self-corroborative human device is the hand — the thumb opposed to four fingers. This ingenious part of the human anatomy allows one to take hold of objects and hold them firmly. A corresponding mechanical tool is the plumber's vise. Any plumber knows the workings of the familiar self-corroborative device anchored to his work bench. It consists of two jaws, one stationary and one movable, with which the plumber gets a firm grip on pipes and other objects with which he is working. But what would happen if either of the jaws were missing? If the stationary jaw were missing, one could screw the movable jaw all the way to the South Pole and never catch hold of anything. On the other hand, if the movable jaw were missing . . . I think you get the point.

Jesus used this same dynamic in making his claim of deity.

No event better illustrates Jesus' use of this dynamic than the healing of the paralytic recorded in Matthew 9:2-8, Mark 2:1-12 and Luke 5:18-26. Mark's account reads:

> A few days later, when Jesus again entered Capernaum, the people heard that he had come home. So many gathered that there was no more room left, not even outside the door, and he preached to them. Some men came, bringing to him a paralytic, carried by four of them. Since they could not get him to Jesus because of the crowd, they made an opening in the roof above Jesus and, after digging through it, lowered the mat the paralyzed man was lying on. When Jesus saw their faith, he said to the paralytic, "Son, your sins are forgiven."
>
> Now some of the teachers of the law were sitting there, thinking to themselves, "Why does this fellow talk like that? He's blaspheming! Who can forgive sins but God alone?"
>
> Immediately Jesus knew in his spirit that this was what they were thinking in their hearts, and he said to them, "Why are you thinking these things? Which is easier, to say to the paralytic, 'Your sins are forgiven,' or to say, 'Get up, take your mat and walk?' But that you may know that the Son of Man has authority on earth to forgive sins . . ." He said to the paralytic, "I tell you, get up, take your mat and go home." And he got up, took his mat and walked out in full view of them all. This amazed everyone and they praised God, saying, "We have never seen anything like this!" (Mk. 2:1-12).

Note the approach Jesus used: he based what could not be proved (his claim to forgive sins) upon what could not be denied (his healing of the paralytic). The very nature of a claim demands evidence other than itself. Claims are, after all, only words. In and of themselves they do not possess the necessary ingredient to be either proved or disproved. Argument won't settle claims; only evidence will. Had Jesus been less than what he was, he would have been forced simply to argue the point in question. When his opponents asserted, "You can't forgive sins," he could only have retorted, "I can too!" Such an argument could not have been resolved because claims cannot be settled in a vacuum. In saying to the paralytic, "Take up your mat and go home," Jesus provided the evidence that ended all argument. In effect, he placed his adversaries squarely in the breach between what would not be proved and what could not be denied.

You can see why such a line of reasoning is pertinent to this study of the life of Jesus and is the thesis of this book. The unbelievable things about Jesus must be viewed in the context of the undeniable things about him. Only in the tension between what is claimed and what is demonstrated can a person find sufficient evidence to support a reasonable conclusion regarding the person of Jesus. The gospel records are full of this type of self-corroborative material that will allow us, like the plumber or the observers of Schliemann's excavations, to take hold of our subject with a firm grip. The records contain the necessary ingredients for bringing the reader to a satisfactory conclusion. They provide sufficient evidence by which the identity of Jesus can be established.

What are the two opposing "jaws" in the gospel materials that allow one to come to grips with the identity of Jesus? They are materials I refer to as the *"Unbelievables"* and the *"Undeniables."* They work as counter forces to each other and produce a dilemma out of which a conclusion can reasonably be drawn. By the use of these materials one can determine either the adequacy or inadequacy of the evidence and thus validate or invalidate it. The remainder of the book is devoted to this task.

The term **Undeniables** is applied to those aspects of Jesus' life and teachings which are so obviously valid, valuable and vital that even Jesus' critics are forced to admit they are true. They are the many things he did and taught which have become the "given," the norm for believer and unbeliever alike; things we would not live without if we could, and could not live without if we would. They are the warp and woof of life as the Western world knows it. The many secular illustrations, both ancient and modern, which will be presented amply confirm these undeniables as an unmovable backdrop against which the "unbelievable" aspects of Jesus' life will be viewed. This section of material will be discussed under the headings, *Impressive Methods, Impeccable Teachings* and *Imposing Philosophy*. We will explore five important concepts which occupy the majority of Jesus' teachings, plus the *Imposing Philosophy* of love which served as the basis for all Jesus taught. We then will consider the significance of Jesus' *Impelling Relationships*.

By the term **Unbelievables** I have in mind those super-human events recorded of Jesus that claim for him powers outside our experience and which caused his early disciples to regard him as divine. This section of material will be discussed under two major headings:

First, under *Jesus' Signs* we will look at some thirty-five separate, out-of-the-ordinary deeds that were the stock and trade of Jesus' ministry. Those deeds were done, allegedly, in the presence of his disciples and other eyewitnesses. They were primary evidence for those eyewitnesses. They are secondary evidence for the rest of us, and, because they are so completely removed from our own experience, they constitute a hurdle to faith.

Second, under *Jesus' Claims,* we will notice approximately one hundred astonishing statements Jesus made about himself. Like the signs, these claims are so interwoven in the fabric of the gospel narrative they cannot be extracted or ignored without destroying the whole record. They, therefore, must be considered an authentic part of the record — and a significant part, since it was Jesus' claims that eventually provided his enemies with what they considered adequate cause to execute him.

The Dilemma asks the ultimate question: "Is Jesus *Legend, Liar, Lunatic,* or *Lord?*" One cannot remain neutral about Jesus. That he lived, no knowledgeable person can deny; how and why he lived, no honest person can ignore.

The **Conclusion** tells a brief story about freedom and makes application to the present investigation.

1. Pool, Lynn and Gray, *One Passion, Two Loves* (New York: Thomas Y. Crowell Company, 1966).

2. Irving Stone, *The Greek Treasure* (New York: Doubleday & Company, 1975), publisher's comment.

3. Ibid., p. 34.

4. Pool, Op. cit., Publisher's comment.

5. Stone, Op. cit., p. 37.

6. Schliemann was a walking contradiction, and this brief account of the Schliemann saga is far too simply told. For the conflict, contradictions and confusion which accompanied Schliemann, personally, and his ten year span of the excavation of Troy see: Michael Wood, *In Search of the Trojan War* (New York: New American Library, Plume Books, 1985). On page 50, Wood recognized that Schliemann "could indeed be unscrupulous; he cheated and lied to get his way; he was surreptitious and conniving; he sometimes dug in secret and purloined material; he smuggled his Trojan treasures abroad rather than give them to the Turks; he desperately craved acceptance by the academic world as a serious scholar and archaeologist, and yet, we now know, he lied about something as trivial as the provenance of some inscriptions he had bought in Athens." Wood, however, concluded, "All this is admitted — and may be thought damning enough. But set against this are the record of the finds in the books and journals and the brilliant letters to *The Times,* and of course the amazing finds themselves. . . . Wayward, naive, enthusiastic, unashamedly romantic, easy to hurt and anxious to learn, Schliemann is a bundle of contradictions; but the judgement on him should be made on the basis of his finds. It was his luck — or skill — to achieve the greatest archaeological discoveries ever made by one person."

7. Stone, Op. cit., p. 37.

8. Ibid., p. 205.

9. Ibid., p. 211.

10. According to Wood (*In Search of the Trojan War,* p. 50) Sophie Schliemann was not with Henry at the time of this discovery. She was not even in Turkey at the time. Schliemann concocted this enhancement to 'encourage her interest in archaeology by including her . . .'

11. Cedric Boulter, "Heinrich Schliemann," *Academic American Encyclopedia* (Danbury, Conn.: Grolier Incorporated, 1984).

12. Wilhelm Dorpfeld, *Troja and Ilion* (Athens, Greece, 1902), as quoted by Wood: *In Search of the Trojan War,* p. 91.

SECTION II
THE
UNDENIABLES

If you are inexperienced in exploring unknown territories—especially the type we are attempting to traverse in this present expedition—we had best explore first some of the less threatening caverns of evidence. In these beginning explorations we will give close attention to those evidences, drawn from both gospel and secular sources, which should find ready confirmation in the reader's heart. We will reserve the difficult passages and deep waters for later consideration.

4

Impressive Methods

No single influence has more greatly affected the moral and ethical standards of the world than Jesus of Nazareth. From his contemporaries who were "amazed at his teaching, because he taught as one who had authority . . ." (Matt. 7:28-29),·to the soldiers who, when ordered to arrest him, returned empty handed with the explanation, "No one ever spoke the way this man does" (John 7:46), to many today who are confronted by Jesus — one thing is certain: Jesus of Nazareth is at least singularly unique, timely, timeless and, acclaimed by both friend and foe alike, an elevating influence of the highest order.

Speaking at a time when admiration of Jesus had long been unpopular among his contemporaries, Adolph Harnack delivered a series of lectures at the University of Berlin (winter semester, 1899-1900) on "The Essence of Christianity" in which he said of Jesus, "We may take up what relation to him we will: in the history of the past no one can refuse to recognize that it was he who raised humanity to this [highest] level. . . . Once more let it be said: we may assume what position we will in regard to him and his message, certain it is that thence onward the value of our race is enhanced."[1]

In 1835 there appeared on the Continent a book which, reportedly, was destined to deal the deathblow to Christianity. It was Strauss' *Life of Jesus,* an in-depth study filled with probing analyses and piercing questions. The book with its outspoken skepticism initially sent shock waves throughout Europe. Yet, with all his effort to demythologize the records and strip them of all supernatural implications, Strauss, at the very end of his work, makes this bold statement:

> . . . this unity [of God and man] is the fundamental basis achieved by Christ, above which piety by nature cannot possibly lift itself to a higher level. . . . The unity of God and man has not appeared in human self-consciousness with any greater creative power than in Jesus, having penetrated and transfigured his entire life uniformly and without perceptible darkness. . . . He is the one who . . . remains unique and unequaled in world history.[2]

Thus even would-be detractors find themselves paying tribute to the moral excellence of Jesus' life and ethic. Whatever else may be denied him, the excellence of Jesus' life is unassailable, and the quality of his teachings unimpeachable.

Scores of his sayings are so relevant and applicable to life they have become virtually universal axioms. Reflecting on these obvious teachings, E. M. Blaiklock observed:

> They rise out of the ancient text, invade other centuries, carry their continuing conviction. They should seem quaint, out of touch, but they do not. They should seem impracticable, but they do not: every age has seen men and women of every nation put them successfully to the test. They should seem remote from common life, but they are not: all time has seen multitudes find in Christ a center for ordinary living, a light for common day. They should seem alien, ancient, Jewish, but they are not: Christ is universal as no other person in history.[3]

The obviousness of Jesus' teachings is seen in their context as well as in their content. By context I mean the raw material out of which his teachings were formed and the circumstances in which they were set.[4] Harry Emerson Fosdick spoke of the down-to-earthness of Jesus' teachings:

> Here in the gospels are vineyards surrounded by hedges and guarded by towers; fields, sometimes beautiful with flowers, sometimes overgrown with thorns. Here are fig trees, needing cultivation, herbs such as mint and rue, and, as well, tares and dry grass in primitive home ovens. Here are pits into which an animal might fall, and houses, made of clay bricks, in danger from downpouring rain. Along the Jordan are reeds shaken by the wind and on the uplands mustard trees in which birds make their nests. Here are all the

typical animals of Palestine — foxes, wolves, dogs, calves, asses, oxen, goats, kids, sheep and lambs. Here vultures gather about their prey, sparrows fall, and ravens, doves, hens and chickens are familiar. Here the farmer, the husbandman, the shepherd go about their daily tasks, businessmen make their investments and artisans ply their trades.[5]

The context of Jesus' teaching was the real world where real people led real lives and experienced real needs.

Some years ago my wife and I and our three sons spent a month in Israel, walking the roads Jesus walked and seeing the sights Jesus saw. We ate in houses resembling those of two thousand years ago and marvelled at the ancient baking methods still in use. We regretfully declined to drink water drawn from wells four thousand years old. We gleaned in their fields, experienced the hospitality of the common folk and witnessed the shrewdness of the shopkeepers. We fished and swam in the Sea of Galilee, walked from Tiberias to Capernaum and drove through Cana. We spent a week in Nazareth, another in Jerusalem. We drove down the main street of Jericho and thought of Zacchaeus and Bartimaeus. We visited Magdala, the home of Mary Magdalene. We bought a blanket in Bethlehem. We walked through the Mount of Olives and examined Roman olive trees so old they were bearing olives when Jesus was alive. The historical and geographical context which cradles Jesus' teachings is so real it shouts confidently: "It is all too consistent with the Gospels to leave any doubt about the factual basis of the record."[6]

Then again, there is a "simplicity and plainness about the stories in the Gospels, which further commends them. It is remarkable how little of the adjective there is — no compliment, no eulogy, no heroic touches, no sympathetic turn of phrase, no great passages of encomium or commendation."[7] There is no attempt to play on the emotions. Even Jesus' execution is reported with such objectivity that the reader is left with the distinct impression that the records were not fabricated to excite, but merely reported to inform: "When they had crucified him, they divided up his clothes by casting lots. And sitting down they kept watch over him there" (Matt. 27:35-36).

But as we look at the things about Jesus which we describe as "obvious," we need to recognize that in the expression "obvious" there is implied a universally accepted basis of judgment. C. S. Lewis, in *Mere Christianity,* noted the existence of such a consensus when he observed how people argued over what was "right" or "wrong," "fair" or "unfair":

> It looks, in fact, very much as if both parties had in mind some kind of Law or rule of fair play or decent behaviour or morality or whatever you like to call it, about which they really agreed. And they have. If they had not, they might, of course, fight like animals, but they could not quarrel in the human sense of the word. Quarreling means trying to show that the other man is in the wrong. And there would be no sense in trying to do that unless you and he had some sort of agreement as to what Right and Wrong are; just as there would be no sense in saying that a footballer had committed a foul unless there was some agreement about the rules of football.[8]

Norman Geisler illustrates the presence of universal standards with the story about a young college student who submitted a paper denying there were any absolute moral principles.[9] The quality of the research and writing was exceptional — definitely an "A" paper. However, upon receiving back the paper, the student saw written across the front: "F — I do not like blue folders."

The student was incensed! He stormed into the professor's office protesting, "This is not fair! It's unjust! I should be graded on the content of my paper, not on the color of the folder!"

The professor smiled and inquired, "Isn't this the paper that argued so forcefully that there are no such objective moral principles as justice and fairness? Did you not argue that everything is simply a matter of one's likes and dislikes?"

"Well, yes," the student replied.

"Then," said the professor, "I do not like blue folders. The grade is "F."

The young man suddenly got the point. Although he had been unaware of it, he did in fact believe in the objective principles of fairness and justice. The lesson having been learned, the professor changed the grade to an "A."

D. M. Baillie refers to "things which are so fundamental that they have no foundations . . . what everyone knows, if only one is willing to know it . . . the inward voice which all can hear . . . which expresses itself in all our values."[10] This universal, comprehensive sentiment lies at the heart of the term "obvious." The obviousness of Jesus' teachings is rooted in what people "already [know] because it lives in the inmost parts of their souls."[11]

In this vein, the observation by Elton Trueblood is appropriate: "After nearly two thousand years, [Jesus] is still the Great Disturber. To this day it is difficult to read His words and still be satisfied with one's own life."[12] It is perhaps for this reason that Jesus of Nazareth, not Julius Caesar nor any one else, has been recognized as the dividing point in history. "To date all documents from Julius Caesar would be ridiculous," concludes Trueblood, "because that would over-glorify the patently local, but about Christ there is an obvious universality. We can be grateful for the rationality of *Anno Domini.* All our dating, whether B.C. or A.D., is a tacit acknowledgment that a significant fact about any other event in history is whether it happened before or after His coming."[13] As we approach the year 2,000 A.D., one question will rise above the celebration: "2,000 years since what?"

How has the man Jesus continued through nearly two thousand years to be the Great Disturber? Lord Beaverbrook, in his book, *The Divine Propagandist,* says, "Jesus now stands before us simply and nakedly as the greatest propagandist the world has ever known. . . . The main . . . weapons used [were] personality, example and oratory. His message was a personal one conveyed in the spoken word."[14] T. R. Glover in attempting to explain Jesus' continuing influence on the hearts of people, observed, "It is commonplace with those who take literature seriously that what is to reach the heart must come from the heart; and the maxim may be applied conversely — that what has reached a heart has come from a heart — that what continues to reach the heart among strange peoples in distant lands, after long ages, has come from a heart of no common make."[15]

How, exactly, did Jesus manage to escape the mark and boundary of his own time and speak with such living vigor and relevance that he was able to span time and place and, indeed, after long ages continue to reach the heart of "strange people in distant lands?" For one thing, Jesus used sound educational methods.[16] "In his 'school' there was created a learning atmosphere. The disciples enjoyed the elements of fellowship and freedom of thought. Jesus employed the Socratic question and answer method by which students were drawn into dialogic encounters with himself and with one another. He taught with clarity, using language the people could understand. . . . And, in keeping with the best educational methods of teaching, he stimulated his disciples to think for themselves, to form positive convictions, and to act accordingly."[17]

Jesus employed two principal elements as he spoke in his unique way to the heart of man. The more obvious and easily defined of the two was the parable. He used it constantly. According to Matthew, "Jesus spoke all these things to the crowd in parables, and he did not say anything to them without using a parable" (13:34). The parables, though little understood initially (Matt. 13:13), were long remembered, as is any vivid story. Jesus wove his parables out of the everyday events of life. Out of the rich backlog of universal human experience he told simple, earthly stories that had a heavenly meaning. He usually began by saying, "The kingdom of heaven is like . . .;" and then proceeded to relate something everyone knew to something he alone seemed to know. And the common people heard him gladly. Everyone loves a story.

Jesus often used short parables: "The kingdom of heaven is like a mustard seed, which a man took and planted in his field. Though it is the smallest of all seeds, yet when it grows, it is the largest of garden plants and becomes a tree, so that the birds of the air come and perch in its branches" (Matt. 13:31, 32).

And even shorter ones: "The kingdom of heaven is like yeast that a woman took and mixed into a large amount of flour until it worked all through the dough" (Matt. 13:33).

He also told longer, more detailed parables:

A farmer went out to sow his seed. As he was scattering the seed, some fell along the path, and the birds came and ate it up. Some fell on the rocky places, where it did not have much soil. It sprang up quickly, because the soil was shallow. But when the sun came up, the plants were scorched, and they withered because they had no root. Other seed fell among the thorns, which grew up and choked the plants. Still other seed fell on good soil, where it produced a crop — a hundred, sixty or thirty times what was sown. (Matt. 13:3-8).

And Jesus seemed always willing to explain in private to his disciples the meaning of his parables. After hearing the parable of the farmer and the seed, Jesus' disciples asked him to explain it. So he said, "Listen then to what the parable of the sower means:"

When anyone hears the message about the kingdom and does not understand it, the evil one comes and snatches away what was sown in his heart. This is the seed sown along the path. What was sown on rocky places is the man who hears the word and at once receives it with joy. But since he has no root, he lasts only a short time. When trouble or persecution comes because of the word, he quickly falls away. What was sown among the thorns is the man who hears the word, but the worries of this life and the deceitfulness of wealth choke it, making it unfruitful. But what is sown on good soil is the man who hears the word and understands it. He produces a crop, yielding a hundred, sixty or thirty times what was sown. (Matt. 13:18-23).

At times Jesus involved his audience in the creation of a parable. One such occasion was the story about the wicked tenants who refused to give the owner of the vineyard his rightful profit. They abused his servants who came to collect and finally killed the owner's son and confiscated the vineyard. Having aroused his hearers' righteous indignation at the tenants' outrageous conduct, he solicited their help in condemning it: "When therefore the owner of the vineyard comes, what will he do to those tenants?" His audience of chief priests and Pharisees, not knowing they were signing their own eviction notice, replied: "He will bring those wretches to a wretched end, and will rent the vineyard to other tenants, who will give him his share of the crop at harvest time" (Matt. 21:33-43).

One of Jesus' parables seems to have been told out of amazement at the fickle nature of the people. Jesus said, "To what, then, can I compare the people of this generation? What are they like? They are like children sitting in the marketplace and calling out to each other: 'We played the flute for you and you did not dance; we sang a dirge, and you did not cry.' For John the Baptist came neither eating bread nor drinking wine, and you say, 'He has a demon.' The Son of Man came eating and drinking, and you say, 'Here is a glutton and a drunkard, a friend of tax collectors and sinners' " (Luke 7:31-34).

At the conclusion of his parables Jesus often would challenge his hearers with a familiar word of encouragement: "He who has ears, let him hear" (Matt. 13:9).

Read any of Jesus' parables, and you'll see they all were constructed out of the materials of everyday life. They were not fables. One senses that Jesus lived close to the people, shared their joys and sorrows, knew their thoughts and felt their hurts. He gave the common people a word of hope and the religious leaders a word of warning. All this reaches our heart and has an all-too-unsettling effect for us ever again to be satisfied with our present level of living. He has lifted our eyes.

The other principal ingredient in Jesus' teachings which deserves special attention was his impeccable logic. He used it extensively. It seldom called attention to itself, but it was there, and it was flawless and unanswerable. Like the parable, logic is respected universally. Just as everyone enjoys a story, so everyone recognizes a "checkmate." We get the point; "Touché!"

Whereas the parables often were not understood by the masses (Matt. 13:10-13), Jesus' logic could hardly be missed. Here is an example: In defense of his healing on the Sabbath, Jesus said to his critics, "I did one miracle, and you all are astonished. Yet, because Moses gave you circumcision . . . you circumcise a child on the Sabbath. Now if a child can be circumcised on the Sabbath so that the Law of Moses may not be broken, why are you angry with me for healing the whole man on the Sabbath?" Then he added, "Stop judging by mere appearances, and make right judgment" (John 7:21-24).

Jesus used plenty of "horse sense" logic — speaking of things everyone ought to know; simple to the point of being simplistic. Such rejoinders as, "It is not the healthy who need a doctor, but the sick" (Mark 2:15); "If a kingdom is divided against itself, that kingdom cannot stand" (3:24); "A city on a hill cannot be hid. Neither do people light a lamp and put it under a bowl" (Matt. 5:14, 15) are obvious to all. He also advised settling out of court: "Settle matters quickly with your adversary who is taking you to court. Do it while you are still with him on the way . . ." (5:25).

Of all the logic Jesus employed, the most touching is that which he used to surround a defenseless person with protection and to shield a friend from the arrows of criticism. One such occasion happened on the Saturday night before his death. Jesus was attending a dinner in his honor at the home of Simon the leper. During the dinner, Mary of Bethany took a flask of expensive perfume (worth a year's wages) and lovingly poured it on Jesus. His disciples began to carp and criticize the extravagance. "Leave her alone," said Jesus. "Why are you bothering her? She has done a beautiful thing to me. The poor you will always have with you, and you can help them any time you want. But you will not always have me. She did what she could. She poured perfume on my body beforehand to prepare for my burial" (Mark 14:6-8).

Jesus' logic varied as the occasion demanded. His most pointed and exposing arguments which laid bare the hypocrisy of his adversaries were reserved for the last week of his life when the battle lines were drawn and the fight was hot and heavy. On one such occasion the Pharisees and the Herodians sent their disciples to trap Jesus in his words:

> "Teacher," they said, "we know you are a man of integrity and that you teach the way of God in accordance with the truth. You aren't swayed by men, because you pay no attention to who they are. Tell us then, what is your opinion. Is it right to pay taxes to Caesar or not?"
>
> But Jesus, knowing their evil intent, said, "You hypocrites, why are you trying to trap me? Show me the coin used for paying the tax." They brought him a denarius . . .
>
> And he asked them, "Whose portrait is this? And whose inscription?"
>
> "Caesar's," they replied.
>
> Then he said to them, "Give to Caesar what is Caesar's, and to God what is God's."
>
> When they heard this, they were amazed. So they left him and went away (Matt. 22:15-22).

Jesus was also a master at turning the tables on his detractors. While the Pharisees were assembled, Jesus asked them,

> "What do you think about the Christ? Whose son is he?"
>
> "The son of David," they replied.
>
> He said to them, "How is it then that David, speaking by the Spirit, calls him 'Lord'? For he says,
>
>> 'The Lord said to my Lord:
>> Sit at my right hand
>>   until I put your enemies under your feet.'
>
> If then David calls him 'Lord,' how can he be his son?" (Matt. 22:41-45).

Scattered throughout the records are many more examples of Jesus' keen logic, but most of these are concentrated in the last four chapters of each of the Synoptics. Two indicators help us recognize these. First, whenever you see a Pharisee tied in a knot, the chances are excellent that immediately preceding it you will find an example of Jesus' keen logic. Second: Whenever you see the common folk slapping their knees in laughter, or with their mouths open in amazement, you can be fairly confident Jesus had once more silenced his opponents. "Touché!"

Speaking of humorous logic,[18] I imagine it was quite a while before Jesus could restore order after he painted the inconsistencies of the religious leaders in this vivid picture: "You blind guides! You strain out a gnat but swallow a camel" (Matt. 23:24). Or the time he described the hypercritical person as someone with a two-by-four jutting out of his eye while he attempts to remove a speck from his neighbor's eye (Luke 6:41, 42). The Arabs have a saying, "He is the best speaker who turns the ear into an eye." Jesus was a master at doing this with a colorful touch of humor.

But there was no humor in Jesus' logic as he came down to the finish. His life was at stake. The lives of his countrymen were in grave danger. A brief forty years would witness the total destruction of Jerusalem by the Roman army under General Titus. The religious leaders were the "blind leading the blind," and Jesus could see the ditch into which the nation was about to fall. So Jesus pulled out all the stops on the Tuesday morning of his last week. What scathing denunciation of hypocrisy and religious abuse! What penetrating insights! His logic was at its best under fire. Time was short — too short to mince words.

"Woe to you, teachers of the law and Pharisees, you hypocrites! You shut the kingdom of heaven in men's faces. You yourselves do not enter, nor will you let those enter who are trying to" (Matt. 23:13).

"Woe to you, teachers of the law and Pharisees, you hypocrites! You travel over land and sea to win a single convert, and when he becomes one, you make him twice as much a son of hell as you are!" (23:15).

"Woe to you, blind guides! You say, 'If anyone swears by the temple, it means nothing; but if anyone swears by the gold of the temple, he is bound by his oath.' You blind fools! Which is greater: the gold, or the temple that makes the gold sacred?

"You say, 'If anyone swears by the altar, it means nothing; but if anyone swears by the gift on it, he is bound by his oath.' You blind men! Which is greater: The gift, or the altar that makes the gift sacred? Therefore, he who swears by the altar swears by it and by everything on it. And he who swears by the temple swears by it and by the one who dwells in it. And he who swears by heaven swears by God's throne and by him who sits on it" (23:16-23).

"Woe to you, teachers of the law and Pharisees, you hypocrites! You clean the outside of the cup and dish, but inside they are full of greed and self-indulgence. Blind Pharisee! First clean the inside of the cup and dish, and then the outside also will be clean" (23:25, 26).

"Woe to you, teachers of the law and Pharisees, you hypocrites! You build tombs for the prophets and decorate the graves of the righteous. And you say, 'If we had lived in the days of our forefathers, we would not have taken part with them in shedding the blood of the prophets.' So you testify against yourselves that you are the descendants of those who murdered the prophets. Fill up, then, the measure of the sin of your forefathers. You snakes! You brood of vipers! How will you escape being condemned to hell?" (23:29-33).

Such articulate denunciation calls to mind Lord Beaverbrook's observation that Jesus' oratory was cumulative in character and increased in intensity as it proceeded until ultimately it reached a tone not far removed from violence. "Thus, the campaign which began with the Sermon on the Mount ends with the expulsion of the moneychangers from the Temple under the threat of mob-riot."[19]

Something within us responds to the insightful parables and the keen logic Jesus used to convey his message. It matters not our nationality or color, whether we are literate or illiterate, rich or poor, male or female, young or old, ancient or modern. If, then, so much of Jesus' teaching rings true, and his logic strikes us as forcefully as it seems to have struck his contemporaries, and if we respond to his ethic with the same disturbing sense of conviction which seems to touch people of all ages and rank, are not we forced to acknowledge that here was a man who knew the hearts of men; a man who understood life deeply and saw its dilemmas clearly? Are not we forced to ask the same question his contemporaries asked, "Where did this uneducated Jew gain such wisdom?" As history's most outstanding serendipity, Jesus forces us to reexamine his claims. They may have more validity than we first thought.

1. Adolph Harnack, *What Is Christianity?* (New York: Harper and Brothers, 1957), pp. 68, 70.

2. David Friedrich Strauss, *The Life of Jesus Critically Examined,* ed. Peter C. Hodgson, trans. George Elliot (Philadelphia: Fortress Press, 1972), p. 801.

3. E. M. Blaiklock, *Who Was Jesus?* (Chicago: Moody Press, 1974), p. 82.

4. See Frank Ballard, *The Miracles of Unbelief* (Edinburg: T. & T. Clark, 1900), p. 255, 256.

5. Harry Emerson Fosdick, *The Man From Nazareth* (New York: Harper and Brothers, 1949), p. 41.

6. Ibid.

7. T. R. Glover, *The Jesus of History* (London: Hodder and Stoughton, 1965 edition), p. 22.

8. C. S. Lewis, *Mere Christianity* (New York: The Macmillan Company, 1943), pp. 3, 4.

9. Norman Geisler, "The Collapse of Modern Atheism," in Roy Abraham Varghese, ed., *The Intellectuals Speak Out About God.* (Regnery Gateway, Inc., 1984), p. 147.

10. D. M. Baillie, *Faith In God* (London: Faber and Faber, n.d.), pp. 194, 195.

11. Harnack, Op. cit., p. 68.

12. Elton Trueblood, *A Place To Stand* (New York: Harper and Row, 1969), p. 55.

13. Ibid., p. 43.

14. Lord Beaverbrook, *The Divine Propagandist* (London: Heinemann, 1962), pp. 35-39.

15. Glover, Op. cit., p. 40.

16. See Luther Weigle, *Jesus and the Educational Method* (New York: Abingdon Press, 1939), Chapter 1.

17. Henlee H. Barnette, *Introducing Christian Ethics* (Nashville, TN: Broadman Press, 1961), pp. 42, 43.

18. Elton Trueblood, *The Humor of Christ* (New York: Harper and Row, 1964). This informative and interesting study of Jesus' humor lists thirty humorous passages in the synoptic gospels.

19. Lord Beaverbrook, Op. cit., pp. 35-39.

5

Impeccable Teachings

There was a knock at the door. I answered it and there stood the young Scandinavian who had come to America for a cycling holiday. Enroute he had come to the little town of Searcy, Arkansas, in the foothills of the Ozark mountains where we were living. I greeted him and invited him in. But he had something more than a social call on his mind. He asked if we could go somewhere and talk. I made arrangements and sat down to listen.

The young man looked at me and said, "Mr. Woodroof, I have been an atheist all my adult life, but atheism brought me to the point that I no longer could distinguish between fact and fiction. I couldn't tell what was real from what was imaginary."

He continued, "I had just enough sanity left to make one decision. I decided to put Jesus of Nazareth to the test; to see if he had anything to say that made sense."

Then he looked at me, quite unembarrassed, and said,

"Everything Jesus taught, that I could test, proved to be 100 percent correct."

What is there about Jesus' teachings that caused the young man to conclude, "Jesus is 100 percent correct?" We have already seen that Jesus' methods were time-tested and educationally sound. And we have seen that the materials out of which his teachings were constructed (his true-to-life parables and his impressive logic) were right on target and call us to sober reflection.

But more important is the *content* of Jesus' teachings. Others have used his methods, but no one else has communicated a message with a content like his. In fairness, there are scholars who take exception to such a claim of uniqueness for Jesus' ethic. Joseph Klausner, a Jewish writer, maintained that "throughout the Gospels there is not one item of ethical teaching which cannot be paralleled either in the Old Testament, the Apocrypha, or in the Talmudic and Midrashic literature of the period near to the time of Jesus."[1] And Klausner wasn't far wrong. By Jesus' own admission he made reference to, borrowed from and reinforced the Old Testament ethic (Matt. 5:17-19). But out of that great moral treasure-trove of the Hebrew Scriptures Jesus brought a fresh perspective and an additional dimension which stretched the wineskin of the human conscience to a degree unparalleled by any previous teacher.[2]

What did Jesus teach that has caused such opposition and yet has made such a lasting impression for good? For one thing, he taught morality upon the basis of great ethical principles (which elevate and liberate the human spirit) rather than the standard fare of legalistic rules (which subjugate and enslave). This gave his ethic validity and permanency. "His teaching was confined to eternal values devoid of the legalism and the unscientific views of the universe which were characteristic of his time. Therefore, there is a timelessness in Jesus' ethic which is free from purely local and temporal conditions."[3]

Nowhere is this more obvious than in his Sermon on the Mount. It has been said that the Sermon on the Mount (Matt. 5, 6, 7) is the "essence" of Jesus' teaching, and that the material in Matthew 5:3-12 (known as the Beatitudes) is the "essence of the essence." Jesus' mind — the mindset of his kingdom — is spelled out in these eight sentences. The figure of a prism (through which light is passed and broken down into its component parts) may help express the relationship between Jesus' basic philosophy of love and the various component parts contained in the eight individual sayings of the

Beatitudes. Any catalogue of his teachings which would omit the Beatitudes would be incomplete. So, at the very beginning, we pause to identify what is universally recognized as pivotal to all Jesus' teachings, the essence of the essence, the Beatitudes:

> Blessed are the poor in spirit,
> for theirs is the kingdom of heaven.
> Blessed are those who mourn,
> for they will be comforted.
> Blessed are the meek,
> for they will inherit the earth.
> Blessed are those who hunger and thirst for righteousness,
> for they will be filled.
> Blessed are the merciful,
> for they will be shown mercy.
> Blessed are the pure in heart,
> for they will see God.
> Blessed are the peacemakers,
> for they will be called sons of God.
> Blessed are those who are persecuted because of righteousness,
> for theirs is the kingdom of heaven.

In addition to the Beatitudes (and to Jesus' basic philosophy of love which we will consider in Chapter 9) there are at least five key themes which Jesus addressed repeatedly and which represent the heart and core of his teaching regarding the "kingdom of heaven." When you have seen them you have seen the heart of Jesus. You will have read his mind. You will know what he was about. They are: 1) Human Freedom, 2) The Value of the Individual, 3) Giving as a Lifestyle, 4) Faith and 5) Life Beyond the Present. As you investigate these themes, you will do well to keep in mind the test to which philosopher Will James would submit them: "What sensible difference to anybody will their truth make?"[4]

Human Freedom

Human Freedom is the first major theme Jesus addressed as he went about the countryside calling his hearers to a change of perspective on life. The society in which he lived was dominated by an entrenched, powerful, religious monopoly. Jesus went head-to-head with that religious establishment in his effort to free common people from its grasp. In this regard it is interesting to note that Jesus dealt exclusively with the religious oppression of the Jewish nation, not the political oppression represented by the Roman occupation forces in Israel at the time. There is not an example where Jesus ever addressed the political picture in an attempt to correct it.

. In attempting to discern the reason for this silence, one could correctly surmise that Jesus' kingdom was not of this world (John 18:36). His strategy for all social problems called for the transformation of individual lives which, in turn, would be a leavening influence on whatever social need might exist. His remedy consists of the elevation of the human condition from within.

But could Jesus have been making another point here — that the more intolerable burden his countrymen were bearing was not the political system which had been imposed on them by strangers, but a religious system imposed by their own "blind guides"? Could he have been saying that, whereas the kingdom of heaven could exist under political rule, however adverse, it could not exist under the religious rule of his day; that the religious establishment of his day actually aborted the kingdom? This is precisely what he said: "Woe to you experts in the law, because you have taken away the key to knowledge. You yourselves have not entered, and you have hindered those who were entering" (Luke 11:52). In fact he charged the lawyers and Pharisees with "shutting the kingdom of God in men's faces" (Matt. 23:13).

This robbing the common people of their freedom was accomplished by an elaborate system of legalism — the invisible but oppressive prison into which the Jewish leaders had thrown the common people, shackling them with human restrictions: "Do this," "Don't do that," "Don't eat this," "Don't wear that," "Don't touch that," "Wash that pan," etc. Such a rigid legalism had loaded the Jewish people with burdens far beyond the Law's requirement and had missed the heart of life. Jesus had much to say about such religious dictators who took all the joy out of life. He was in line with the Hebrew prophets who often said to the religious hierarchy of their day: "Give the people a rest; get off their back!" He said, "The teachers of the law and the Pharisees . . . tie up heavy loads and put them on men's shoulders, but they themselves are not willing to lift a finger to move them" (Matt. 23:2-4).

When he saw the massive abuse of the Sabbath law by religious leaders who imposed hundreds of man-made restrictions on the people, Jesus repeatedly called them to task, saying, "The Sabbath was made for man, not man for the Sabbath" (Mark 2:27). On one Sabbath he was criticized for healing a woman who had been deformed for eighteen years. When Jesus saw her, he called her forward and said to her,

> "Woman, you are set free from your infirmity." Then he put his hands on her, and immediately she straightened up and praised God.
>
> Indignant because Jesus had healed on the Sabbath, the ruler of the synagogue said to the people, "There are six days for work. Come and be healed on those days, not on the Sabbath."
>
> Jesus replied: "You hypocrites! Doesn't each of you on the Sabbath untie his ox or donkey from the stall and lead it out to give it water? Then should not this woman, a daughter of Abraham, whom Satan has kept bound for eighteen long years, be set free on the Sabbath day from what bound her?" (Luke 13:10-15).

The legalism of Jesus' day was designed and perpetuated by loop-hole lawyers content to engage in ceremonial hand-washing while depriving their own parents of financial aid. On the excuse of having their money tied up in TSAs (Temple Sheltered Annuities) or ÇDs ("Corban" Deposits), they dishonored their own parents:

"You hypocrites!" said Jesus, "Isaiah was right when he prophesied about you:

> These people honor me with their lips,
>> but their hearts are far from me.
>
> They worship me in vain;
>> their teachings are but rules made by man."
>
> Matt. 15:7-9.

In the hearing of all the people Jesus warned:

> Beware of the teachers of the law. They like to walk around in flowing robes and love to be greeted in the marketplaces and have the most important seats in the synagogues and the places of honor at banquets. They devour widows' houses and for a show make lengthy prayers. Such men will be punished most severely (Luke 20:46, 47).

The tyranny of the legalism of Jesus' day differed little, if any, from the repression and abuses of totalitarian religions of all times. And he would have no part of any of it. He gave his life to bring all such oppression to an end. Repeatedly he endorsed the priority expressed in the Hebrew scriptures, "I desire mercy not sacrifice." At the beginning of his ministry he committed himself to the noble cause of lifting up the disenfranchised and liberating the captive. He went to the synagogue in his home town one day, unrolled the scroll of Isaiah, and read:

> The Spirit of the Lord is on me;
>> therefore he has anointed me to preach the good news to the poor.
> He has sent me to proclaim freedom for the prisoners
>> and recovery of sight for the blind,
> to release the oppressed,
>> to proclaim the year of the Lord's favor.

He then rolled up the scroll, Luke records, gave it back to the attendant and sat down. Everyone's attention in the synagogue was focussed on him, and he said to them, "Today this scripture is fulfilled in your hearing" (Luke 4:18-21). With this bold statement Jesus announced his platform of liberation.

There is a beautiful parallel in our own Statue of Liberty. After a century of lifting her lamp beside the golden door, the "Grand Lady of Liberty" received renewed honor, and her noble motto was reaffirmed:

> Give me your tired, your poor, your huddled masses yearning to breathe free, the wretched refuse of your teeming shore. Send these, the homeless, tempest-tossed to me. I lift my lamp beside the golden door.

Can anyone fail to see the similarity between her motto and Jesus' invitation:

> Come to me, all you who are weary and burdened, and I will give you rest. Take my yoke upon you and learn of me, for I am gentle and humble in heart, and you will find rest for your souls. For my yoke is easy and my burden is light (Matt. 11:28, 29).

No struggle for freedom has been more forcefully brought home to the American people than that of American blacks. They were uprooted unmercifully from their African homeland at the instigation of whites; loaded like lumber aboard slave vessels; and sold like chattel to other whites, some of whom professed to be Christians. Reason would seem to dictate the inescapable conclusion: "Have nothing to do with the white man's God."

Yet when the slaves got a glimpse of Jesus of Nazareth, they pinned their hopes on him. They sorted through the maze of the religious inconsistencies of their captors and came to the conclusion that Jesus understood their plight. From the heart of that oppressed people there came the sound of the soul crying for relief:

> Nobody knows the trouble I've seen, Nobody knows my sorrow.
> Nobody knows the trouble I've seen; Glory, Hallelujah.
> Sometimes I'm up, sometimes I'm down; O, yes, Lord.
> Sometimes I'm almost to the ground, O, yes, Lord.
> Nobody knows the trouble I've seen, Nobody knows but Jesus,
> Nobody knows the trouble I've seen. O, Yes, Lord.

How influential was Jesus in the liberation of American blacks during the 1960s? Martin Luther King Jr., their eloquent leader, was a second generation Baptist preacher who openly patterned his "turn the other cheek" philosophy after Jesus' example. Viewing what he considered the beginning of the end of the oppression of his people, King immortalized mankind's craving for freedom in the words, "Free at last! Free at last! Thank God Almighty, I'm free at last!"

Indirectly, the United States Postal Service acknowledged Jesus' part in the black liberation movement when it issued a special commemorative stamp for February 1986 in honor of the Black race and its struggle for freedom. Printed boldly across the poster advertising the stamp was a portion of a statement of Jesus: *"And the Truth Shall Make You Free."* Jesus spoke the language of freedom and liberty that touches the heart of all people who "yearn to breathe free."

Jesus offended the audience to whom he made the statement, "You will know the truth, and the truth will set you free." They answered him, "We are Abraham's descendants, and have never been slaves of anyone. How can you say we shall be set free?" (John 8:31-33). Yet, knowing Jewish history, that the majority of their national existence prior to the time of Jesus had been spent either as literal captives in foreign lands or as subjects of occupational forces in their own land, it seems incomprehensible that they should boast, "We have never been slaves of anyone."

But in a way they were right. Although one's body may be enslaved, one's spirit can remain free. This great truth has been documented through the years but seldom more effectively than by Victor Frankl, a Jew who survived the Nazi prison camps of World War II and wrote his best-seller out of that experience.[5]

My own life once was touched by Jewish national pride in a way which dramatically illustrates the indomitable Jewish spirit. While in Israel my family and I camped in a grass hut by the Sea of Galilee. Having walked most of the way from Tiberias to Capernaum that day, we were ready for a good night's rest. We prepared our bed rolls and eagerly crawled in. By midnight the Galilean countryside and its American guests had been lulled to sleep by the gentle lapping of waves against the shore.

But suddenly we were startled out of our sleep! Horns blared! Lights glared! Shouting voices split the early morning silence!

I looked at my watch; it was 4:30 A.M. I slung on my clothes, grabbed my tape recorder and headed in the direction of the noise. I was directed by jubilant teens to their adult leader.

"What's happening?" I asked.

The leader explained, "These Scouts have just completed their induction with a seventy-five kilometer trek. Now they're celebrating."

"In about an hour," he said, pointing to an imposing range of mountain cliffs to the west of the Sea, "we're going to drive up to the top of Mt. Arbel for a history lesson."

I couldn't resist. "May I go with you?" I asked.

"Sure," he replied.

At 6 a.m. I climbed into one of the army trucks with about twenty-five teenage Scouts, and we began the jostling journey to the brow of the mountain. There was only one possible approach to the imposing precipice which stood like a sentinel guarding the Sea of Galilee: the western slope which provided a gentle incline. So we drove to the base of the mountain and began our ascent.

When we reached the pinnacle and disembarked, we carefully approached the precipice and looked straight down upon perhaps a thousand feet of crag and gully. To our left stood a ragged mountain range; to our right lay the historic sea of Galilee bathed in the early morning sunlight.

The leader called the group together and began telling of the heroic episode which had involved their ancestors more than two thousand years earlier. Rather than bow to the presence of Rome, so the lesson went, a small group of Jewish patriots secretly stored arms and provisions in the caves tucked in the vertical cliffs near the pinnacle of Mt. Arbel. With ample provisions they held up in the caves and dared Rome to come get them.

The leader beckoned with his hand and we followed, carefully making our way down the face of the precipice into the mouth of one of the caves. There before us was a whole network of caverns still bearing the marks of occupancy by a man named Hezekiah and his followers in the early days of the Roman occupation. Our leader pointed out the munitions room and the kitchen still black from the smoke of many fires.

When this pocket of resistance was discovered Rome dispatched an armed contingent (accompanied by a young Herod — later "the Great," ruler of Judea during 37-4 B.C.) to put down the rebellion. But it did not put down easily. Time after time waves of Roman soldiers attempted to scale the steep face leading up to the fortress. Time after time they were hurled back. More forces were sent; more were killed.

Finally, according to our guide, the Roman soldiers devised a plan of attack from above the precipice, lowering baskets of soldiers armed sufficiently to subdue the rebels. When the end was near, before the final onslaught, Herod stood below the fortress and appealed to Hezekiah, whom Josephus describes as "a certain old man, the father of seven children . . .", to surrender. Hezekiah's children also, "together with their mother, desired him to give them leave to go out, upon the assurance and right hand that was offered them." But Hezekiah refused and began to carry out a desperate plan — the systematic execution of his whole family:

> He ordered every one of them to go out, while he stood himself at the cave's mouth, and slew [each] son of his . . . who went out. Herod was near enough to see this sight, and his bowels of compassion were moved at it, and he stretched out his right hand to the old man, and besought him to spare his children; yet he did not relent at all upon what he said, but over and above reproached Herod on the lowness of his descent, and slew his wife as well as his children; and when he had thrown their dead bodies down the precipice, he at last threw himself down after them.[6]

Hezekiah's response is reminiscent of Masada a century later. This is not surprising. After all, Hezekiah was the father of Judas of Galilee (a nationalist rebel against Rome, referred to in Acts 5:37),[7] and the grandfather of Menahem who captured Masada from King Herod in the Jewish war against Rome in A.D. 66. It was Menahem's nephew, Elazar, who commanded the defense of Masada during the Roman siege in A.D. 73 and orchestrated the mass suicide for which Masada has become so well known.[8] It was this spirit of 'live free or die' which prompted the Jews' reply to Jesus: "We are Abraham's descendants and have never been slaves of anyone." And from the Arbel and Masada incidents we are better able to understand what they meant.

But they didn't understand what Jesus meant by freedom. He was calling attention to their need to be free from an even greater enslavement that holds the whole human race under its control: "I tell you the truth, everyone who sins is a slave of sin" (John 8:34). The word "sin" offended the first century Jew as much as the word "Roman." But the presence of sin in their lives was no less real than the presence of Rome, and its power no less total. Just as it was possible for the body to be enslaved yet the spirit be free, so was it possible for the body to be free while the spirit was enslaved to sin.

Jesus' statement, "If you hold to my teaching . . . you will know the truth, and the truth will set you free," provokes a similar response in Americans: "We are Americans, and have never been slaves of anyone!" Yet, with just a moment's reflection, we know that is not a true statement. We are an enslaved people. Alcoholics are not free. Neither addicts nor pushers of marijuana, cocaine, uppers, downers, speed, acid, paint thinner, morphine, tobacco or pornography are free. And what is the justification for this enslavement?

> . . . If we listen we can hear its defense summed up in a single, solitary, grievously misunderstood word: *liberty*. Under the guise of personal freedom, seemingly powerless before the prevailing code, fearful of any absolute except the belief that there are no absolutes, our nation pushes on through increasingly troubled waters, a great ship that is all sail but no rudder. We have at our disposal vast amounts of knowledge and technology, but no sense of direction, no heart and soul. Spurred on by greed and the profit motive, men of low mind and dingy morals ply their seedy trade to the cries of a liberated age: "I'm free! I'm free!" All the while a whole culture, deceived and deceiving, unable or unwilling to intervene, looks the other way. All along the roadside the little ones . . . litter the right-of-way, discarded for the sake of our "freedom" like yesterday's newspaper.[9]

The almighty dollar enslaves, driving millions of Americans to the brink of ruin as they compromise either their scruples or their health to obtain more and more. Lee Iacocca recalls the warning his father gave him about the tyranny of money: "Be careful about money," said the elder Iacocca. "When you have five thousand, you'll want ten. And when you have ten, you'll want twenty." Lee, whose salary for 1985-86 was reported to have been eleven million dollars, agreed: "He was right. No matter what you have, it's never enough."[10]

And how many slaves does Status hold in its control!?

Then there is the "one-eyed Monster" in our homes which controls our minds and lives, arranging our schedules and robbing us of precious hours.

There are also the hidden masters that control and manipulate us and make us vulnerable to all our false gods. There are the demons of hate, jealousy, envy, anger, lust, lying, deception, malice — all henchmen of the Self, carrying out the insidious dictates of his will. To these we daily bow in submission. And, in spite of all we vow, we cannot seem to get free of them. They dominate and rule us; they dictate and ruin us. They make us what we do not want to be and prevent us from being what we know in our heart we ought to be. We are enslaved.

What did Jesus recommend as the solution to such slavery? What did Jesus have in mind when he promised, "If

the Son sets you free, you will be free indeed?" First, he identified the source of the problem: "Out of the heart come evil
thoughts, murder, adultery, sexual immorality, theft, false
testimony, slander. These are what make a man 'unclean'; but
eating with unwashed hands does not make him 'unclean'"
(Matt. 15:19, 20).

While modern attempts to affix blame for the human predicament would rightly laugh at the idea of unwashed hands
being the cause, they tend at the same time to point to yet
other externals: slums, poverty and illiteracy. But even they
are only contributing factors. They are not the source. According to Jesus, the heart is the source of all moral aberrations.
Bertrand Russell, an avowed opponent of Christianity, agrees:
"It is in our hearts that the evil lies, and it is from our hearts
that it must be plucked out."[11]

Jesus had prescribed the same corrective nineteen hundred
years earlier:

> Woe to you, teachers of the law and Pharisees, you hypocrites! You
> clean the outside of the cup and dish, but inside they are full of
> greed and self-indulgence. Blind Pharisee! First clean the inside of
> the cup and dish, and then the outside will also be clean (Matt.
> 23:25, 26).

Accordingly, Jesus taught that murder and adultery are only
the fruits of being enslaved to hate and lust (see Matt. 5:21-28).
And in this perception Jesus was unique. Lofthouse affirms
that Jesus' insistence "on turning from the act which a judge
might deal with, to the motive which lies outside the range of
law finds no parallel in any Jewish writing."[12]

The Value of the Individual

Closely connected to Jesus' concern for human freedom
was his concept of human value, and particularly the value of
the individual. "Jesus Christ was the first to bring the value of
every human soul to light," said Harnack, "and what he did no
one can any more undo."[13] Jesus based this respect for the
individual upon what he claimed was God's respect for the individual. By calling attention to God's faithful feeding of the
birds of the air, Jesus encouraged his hearers not to worry
about the daily needs of life. "Look at the birds of the air," he

would say; "they do not sow or reap or store away in barns, and yet your heavenly Father feeds them. Are you not much more valuable than they?" (Matt. 7:26). He further observed that sparrows, which sold for "two for a penny," were important enough to God that "not one of them will fall to the gound without the will of your Father" (10:29), and that "the very hairs of your head are all numbered" (10:30). "So don't be afraid," he said; "you are worth more than many sparrows" (10:31).

A companion affirmation of human value is found in Jesus' exclamation recorded in Matthew 12:12: "How much more valuable is a man than a sheep!" Jesus knew his Jewish hearers agreed in principle with his teachings on human worth. And so do we. This is why we accept slaughter houses for sheep but react with horror to the slaughter houses for humans which operated in Germany during World War II. The Nuremberg Trials were the combined conscience of the world echoing resolutely in unison with Jesus' affirmation that human beings are not to be treated like sheep.

> What do you think? If a man owns a hundred sheep, and one of them wanders away, will he not leave the ninety-nine on the hills and go to look for the one that wandered off? And if he finds it, I tell you the truth, he is happier about that one sheep than about the ninety-nine that did not wander off. In the same way your Father in heaven is not willing that any of these little ones should be lost (Matt. 18: 12-14).

In a day when humans could be bought for 30 pieces of silver, when slaves were pitted against wild animals in the Roman games, and when undesired infants were the victims of infanticide, Jesus' regard for the individual was a welcome breath of fresh air.

Likewise today, when automation has made humans increasingly expendable, when slaves to drugs are pitted against the wild animals who traffic in them, and when unwanted infants are the victims of abortion, Jesus' regard for the individual is once again a welcome breath of fresh air.

Thus Jesus called for an increased respect for the human individual. He warned against insulting one's fellow man, saying that anyone who said to his brother, 'Raca' (a term of contempt), was answerable to the Sanhedrin court of law. And anyone who said 'You fool!' would be in danger of the fire of hell. Prefacing both of these with a warning against anger (Matt. 5:21, 22), Jesus affirmed that human beings deserve better treatment than that.

Jesus' emphasis on human worth also elevated womanhood. The record indicates that women sensed Jesus' acceptance of them, and many followed him (Matt. 27:55, 56). He spoke respectfully with them in public, making no distinction between male and female. He attempted to liberate women from sexual abuse by condemning pornographic thoughts which reduce women to the status of sex objects: "You have heard that it was said, 'Do not commit adultery,' But I tell you that anyone who looks at a woman lustfully has already committed adultery with her in his heart" (Matt. 5:27, 28). Jesus also affirmed the value of women by strengthening the sanctity of marriage, stating that divorce was not to be "for every cause" (Matt. 19:3), but only if one's partner were sexually unfaithful. Women are still the principal beneficiaries of this restriction.

Jesus' new ethic on individual worth also put a premium on truthfulness. His insistence that a man's word be as good as his bond was rooted in the respect that one human being should have for another. The system of vows practiced among the Jews of Jesus' day was an elaborate network of loop-holes by which the one making the vow could claim release from it through a technicality (Matt. 23:16-22). Jesus said a person should not swear at all, but rather let 'Yes' be 'Yes' and 'No' be 'No.' "Anything beyond this comes from the evil one" (Matt. 5:34-37). In today's world when case after air-tight case is thrown out of court due to a technicality, and contracts are nullified because of some ambiguity in the legalese, it would be refreshing if we could recapture the genuineness Jesus advocated when he said, in effect, 'Let your word be your bond.'

Jesus' teaching on human worth also demanded non-retaliation. The norm had been "an eye for an eye," but Jesus taught, "Do not retaliate at all" (Matt. 5:38-42). Jesus was not advocating the dismantling of the justice system. He was saying that, when injury has been incurred in personal relations, we should neither strike back nor build protective walls around us, but rather "turn the other cheek," and "go the second mile." Human relations today could use a good stiff dose of such advice.

If Jesus' teachings on human freedom and individual worth do not seem obvious to us, perhaps it is because we are viewing them from the standpoint of our granting freedom and worth to others. A simple maneuver will shed new light on the subject: Look at it from the other end. We all want to be treated like Jesus taught people to treat others. We all want to be accorded freedom and worth. That much is obvious! And by this simple equation — "Do to others what you would have them do to you" (Matt. 7:12) — Jesus convicts us of the rightness of his ethic.

1. Joseph Klausner, *Jesus of Nazareth* (New York: Macmillan Co., 1925), p. 384.

2. See H. E. W. Turner, "The Life and Teaching of Jesus Christ," *A Companion to the Bible*, 2nd. edit., ed. T. W. Manson (Edinburgh: T. & T. Clark, 1963), pp. 436-494.

3. Barnette, Op. cit., p. 43.

4. Will James, "Pragmatism," as found in *The Practical Cogitator*, p. 35. Cf. William James, *Essays in Radical Empiricism* (Cambridge, Mass.: Harvard University Press, 1976).

5. Victor Frankl, *Man's Search For Meaning* (New York: Washington Square Press, 1959).

6. Josephus, *Wars*, William Whiston, trans., (Philadelphia: The John C. Winston Company, n.d.), I. 16. 4, p. 632.

7. There seems to be a discrepancy on this point. If Hezekiah killed all of his children at Arbel, how could Judah (leader of a later uprising mentioned in Acts 5:37) be his son? Yet, Josephus explicitly says Hezekiah had a son named Judah who himself led uprisings. See *Antiquities*, XVII. 10. 5, p. 523 (See footnote); also *Wars*, IV. 3. 1, p. 669; *Antiquities*, XVI. 9. 3, p. 420. Perhaps Judah was an older son already away from home at the time of the Arbel resistance during which Hezekiah and remaining family died.

8. Josephus, *Wars*, Op. cit., VII. 8. 6, p. 850. See also Daniel Gavron, *Walking Through Israel* (Boston: Houghton Mifflin Company, 1980), p. 114.

9. Lanny Henninger, "Who Cares For The Children?," *We Preach Christ Crucified*, ed. Jerry Rushford (Malibu, CA: Pepperdine University Press, 1986), p. 26.

10. Lee Iacocca, *Iacocca, An Autobiography* (New York: Bantom Books, 1984), p. 146.

11. Bertrand Russell, *Has Man A Future?* (Harmondsworth: Penguin Books, 1961), p. 110.

12. W. F. Lofthouse, "Biblical Ethics," *A Companion to the Bible*, 1st edit., ed. T. W. Manson (Edinburgh: T. & T. Clark, 1936), p. 360, as quoted in Barnette, Op. cit., p. 44.

13. Harnack, Op. cit., pp. 67, 68.

6

More Impeccable Teachings

Kern rode joyfully atop a buxom stalk of wheat in the warm Kansas sunshine. "Life is great!" he thought, as he took a deep breath, scarcely able to contain himself at all the beauty around him. "It don't get no better than this," he thought.

But suddenly, interrupting his sun bath, a huge, lumbering steel giant with wildly swinging arms heads straight for him.

"Good grief!" Kern thinks, "that idiot is going to run right over me! Somebody help me! I'll be killed! I don't want to die!"

Of course Kern doesn't know it's not the intention of Combine to kill him. Combine explains that he "just wants to put Kern in a nice, dry storage bin, safe from the reach of some hungry cow that might eat him."

"Whew! What a relief!"

Kern is whisked away by a large truck and funneled down a long chute into a dark, but dry, bin. He snuggles down in his new quarters for a long winter's nap.

"Accommodations are a little cramped," he observes. "But I can manage. At least I'm safe; that's the important thing."

It seems he no sooner got settled than the bin door swung open, letting in bright rays of spring sunshine.

"Hey! Shut the door!" Kern shouts. "The light's hurting my eyes. Can't a seed get any rest around here?"

Farmer Brown doesn't even hear him; he continues preparing for spring planting.

"Millie," Farmer Brown calls out to his wife, "I'm going to plant this wheat; I'll be back for supper."

Kern Wheat's ears perk up, and his heart pounds. He nudges a seedy character next to him and asks:

"What does 'plant' mean?"

"Oh," says the other, scratching his husk, "plantin' is a ritual humans go through every spring. They take us seeds, so I'm told — they missed me last year — and throw us down into a deep hole and step on us."

"What?!" Kern protests, "That'll hurt!"

"Not for long," says the old seed. "In a few days, I hear, you die . . . and then the strangest thing happens."

"What?" asks Kern.

The old fella stroked his husk and said in amazement, "A hunerd new ones come up outa ya, just like yaself. It's the darndest thing I ever heard of."

"But I don't want to die," cries Kern.

"I know," says the old seed. "None of us does; but it sure beats sittin' here all alone year after year."

"Yep," says the old seed, "And I heard t'other day that dyin' so others could live is what bein' a seed is all about."

Giving as a Lifestyle

So much for the elaboration on Jesus' statement: "Unless a kernal of wheat falls to the ground and dies, it remains only a single seed. But if it dies, it produces many seeds" (John 12:24).

It doesn't take a smart seed to die and reproduce. It's all programed into it. But humans? That's a different story. We do everything in our power to keep from dying to ourselves. But one is hard pressed to find a subject which occupied more instruction time from Jesus than that of dying to self. It appears under two or three different headings, all related to each other and focused on a third major theme of Jesus: "Giving as a lifestyle."

The crowning statement of all his teachings on giving, strangely enough, is not recorded in the Gospels themselves but in a statement of Paul quoting Jesus:

"It is more blessed to give than to receive" (Acts 20:35).

Think for a moment of all the tight-fisted, penny-pinching, Scrooges you have known who hoarded their money and themselves. Did you ever see a really happy one? No, and I doubt you ever will. In an article entitled "On The Cheap: The Unhappy Life of J. Paul Getty,"[1] *Business Week* magazine reviews the book *The Great Getty* by Robert Lenzner. Though Getty was king over an oil empire that stretched from the Persian Gulf to California and was pursued by beautiful women half his age, Getty, who "had it all" had nothing that really mattered. "Getty," the author charged, "was hardly the sort of swashbuckling character who inspires movie legends. Early on, he turned into a mean-spirited skinflint, a compulsive bargain-hunter able to tolerate only the most superficial human contact. . . . [Getty] led a cold, cheerless existence in which personal tragedy and conflict were commonplace." Author William Glasgall asks the question, "Why was Getty this way?" but offers no answer.

Could it be that Jesus was right when he affirmed that 'a person is happier giving than receiving'? And when he insisted that "whoever finds his life will lose it, and whoever loses his life for my sake will find it" (Matt. 10:39) — could he have been right?

Jesus elaborated on this concept as he and his disciples were traveling near the city of Caesarea Philippi. He began to explain that he must "go to Jerusalem and suffer many things at the hands of the elders, chief priest and the teachers of the law, and that he must be killed . . ." (Matt. 16:21).

The thought of giving to the point of laying down one's life so offended Simon Peter that he took Jesus aside and began to rebuke him:

"Never, Lord," said Peter. "This shall never happen to you."

But Jesus turned and said to Peter: "Out of my sight, Satan! You are a stumbling block to me; you do not have in mind the things of God, but the things of men" (Matt. 16:22,

23). Jesus proceeded to explain to his disciples a principle of life which has come to be recognized as an undisputed axiom: "Whoever wants to save his life shall lose it, but whoever loses his life . . . will find it" (Matt. 16:25). Though millions insist on pursuing the opposite philosophy, those who have devoted themselves to a life of giving know Jesus was right in his assessment. One *is* happier giving than receiving. The joy of giving outlasts the fleeting thrill of receiving. A proverb of India goes so far as to assert, "All that is not given is lost."

Provided one has learned *how* to give.

"Come on," you may be saying, "You mean giving must be done in a certain way for it to be fun?"

That's right. There's an art to giving, and if you miss it, you'll feel ripped off all your giving life (which probably will be brief). In the Sermon on the Mount (Luke 6:27-36) Jesus explained the "how" of giving by describing two very different kinds of giving. One way brings joy; the other brings only sorrow and disappointment. Sadly, the latter of the two is the way most people give.

You know the script: People giving only to those who give to them; speaking only to those who speak to them; loving only those who love them; doing only for those from whom they hope to receive. "You scratch my back, I'll scratch yours." Its the "exchange of gifts" syndrome. It is giving with expectations and agendas attached in which happiness is determined by the response of the receiver; and so often the response of the receiver does not come up to the expectations of the giver.

> If you love those who love you, what credit is that to you? Even 'sinners' love those who love them. And if you do good to those who do good to you, what credit is that to you? Even 'sinners' do that. And if you lend to those from whom you expect repayment, what credit is that to you? Even 'sinners' lend to 'sinners' expecting to be repaid in full (Luke 6:32-34).

The word "expecting" jumps off the page and thumbs its nose at all of us who have spent our lives giving with expectation written all over our face. But if we'll think for a moment, we'll know that our expectations are seldom fulfilled. More often than not we walk away with disappointment written all over our same face. How many relationships have been destroyed because one partner did not respond to the level of the expectation of the other. There's got to be a better way.

I once explored the better way with a troubled woman. She was about forty years old, this lady who came hesitantly to my office. Her life was in shambles, her marriage was on the rocks. When she realized I would listen she began dumping all the bad news about her husband and his cloddish insensitivity to her. I listened for about an hour. When we both were about knee deep in garbage, I asked her a question:

"I'll bet you give in a lot to him, don't you?"

I shouldn't have asked, because she opened another bag of pent-up garbage and started dumping it also.

"All I do is give in!" she blurted out. She gave example after example. I listened until the garbage was about waist deep, and then I gave her the following instruction:

"Don't ever give in to your husband again."

"What do you mean?" she asked, visibly puzzled.

"Just what I said," I replied. "Don't ever give in to him again . . . ever!" She was now dubious of my sanity. I explained:

"You must stop giving *in* to him . . . and start *giving.*"

What a difference there is! Giving in belittles the other person; giving affirms. Giving in takes away; giving bestows. Giving in says, "I tolerate you"; giving says, "I love you." Giving in causes restentment; giving brings happiness and joy.

A light seemed to turn on in her brain; it showed in her eyes as she said, somewhat startled, "I can do that. I've done it to others, and it worked; I don't know why I've never thought of doing it to my husband." And she walked out determined to start practicing the second kind of giving Jesus described:

> But I tell you . . . Love your enemies, do good to them, and lend to them without expecting to get anything back. Then your reward will be great, and you will be sons of the Most High, because he is kind to the ungrateful and wicked. Be merciful, just as your Father is merciful (Luke 6:35, 36).

"Without expecting to get anything back." Today we call it "giving with no strings attached." This means that one is to give simply because giving, in itself, is good. One's motive for giving is the well-being of the receiver — and that alone. Relationships grow and deepen only if "no strings" giving is practiced. Jesus was right!

*   *   *   *   *   *

The teachings of Jesus on giving are one and the same as his teachings on serving. The guidelines for one are the guidelines for the other, because serving is merely the giving of ourselves to those who need us. Jesus connected the two when he said, "The Son of Man did not come to be served, but to serve, and to give his life as a ransom for many" (Matt. 20:28). Thus he could with authority call his followers to the same kind of servant life-style.

> Then Jesus called them together and said, "You know that the rulers of the Gentiles lord it over them, and their officials exercise authority over them. Not so with you. Instead whoever wants to become great among you must be your servant, and whoever wants to be first must be your slave" (Matt. 20:25-27).

I don't know how the idea of servanthood sets with you, but a quick glance at the sales charts of books such as *Winning Through Intimidation, How To Get The Upper Hand,* and *Getting Your Way* indicates that many people are traveling in the opposite direction. But that direction is a no-win situation. Those who get to the top by stepping on the people around them will find it awfully lonesome when they get where they are going. The really great people are discovering that Jesus was right when he called leaders first to be servants.[2]

Senator Mark Hatfield of Oregon stated his convictions on this matter: "My whole understanding of leadership and power underwent a fundamental change as I searched out my future." He stated that power and prestige could not be the goals which gave his life direction or purpose: "No longer could I define leadership in terms of holding positions of power. Further, power in its truest sense was not political muscle, influence, and public prestige. I was coming to a whole new understanding of what power truly is. . . . Service to others, solely for their own behalf and even entailing deep sacrifice, is the true essence of leadership and the ultimate form of power."[3]

*   *   *   *   *   *

Add to the subjects of giving and serving the subject of forgiving. Leo Buscaglia identifies forgiveness as one of the three essential ingredients in successful human relationships.[4] On the same occasion when Jesus taught, "Lend without expecting to get anything back," he also said, "Love your enemies, do good to those who hate you, bless those who curse you, pray for those who mistreat you" (Luke 6:27, 28). Of course this is not possible unless forgiveness has been extended to the offender. That's a bitter pill for some to swallow.

But what is our option? The only alternative is to harbor hate and animosity and carry grudges to our grave like a quarry slave driven to his dungeon. An anonymous writing describes the slavery hate imposes:

HOW TO BE A SLAVE

Hate somebody! The moment you start hating a man you become his slave. He controls your thoughts, invades your dreams, absorbs your creativity and determines your appetite. He affects your digestion, robs you of your peace of mind . . . and takes away the pleasure of your work . . . You can't get away from the man you hate. He is with you awake or asleep; he invades your privacy when you eat. He influences even the tone of your voice when you speak to your boss, your wife or child. He requires you to take medicine for indigestion, headaches and loss of memory. He steals time and dissipates energy. You want to be a slave? Find somebody and hate him.[5]

A short story in a *Reader's Digest* some years ago suggested a workable alternative. It told about a man who took a friend with him to buy a newspaper.

"Whadaya want?" growled the newsstand attendant.

The man answered politely, "Today's newspaper, please." And he gave the attendant his money.

The attendant thrust the paper at him, took the money and, without a word, turned away.

"Thank you," said the customer.

There was no reply.

As they walked away, the friend asked, "Does he always act like that?"

"He has for about the last ten years," the man said.

The friend asked again, "Have you always treated him like you just did?"

"I have for about the last ten years," was the reply.

The friend shook his head in disbelief. "I don't understand," he said.

The man who bought the paper explained: "I'm not going to let that man determine how I act."

Forgiveness is the only way to set us free from the hurts and hassels thrown at us by wounded people. Peter once asked Jesus:

"How many times shall I forgive my brother when he sins against me? Up to seven times?"

Jesus answered, "I tell you, not seven times, but seventy times seven" (Matt. 18:21-22).

If you have ever experienced the joy of giving to another, the fulfillment of serving another, and the release which comes from forgiving another, you'll know Jesus was right when he prescribed this life-style as the only way to live.

Faith

Faith is another of Jesus' major themes. Some people reject the whole idea of faith, saying, "I don't live my life by faith; I base my life on facts only."

But take another look. Practically all of life is lived in faith. Simple actions (such as drinking water from a tap) are regulated by faith. We don't test each glass of water to guarantee it hasn't been poisoned. Based on our past experience we drink the water "in faith" that it is safe. We also eat food without hiring a food taster. Though some paranoid monarchs of the past believed they could not approach life so trustingly, we don't live like that. We trust our spouses not to poison us. We concede the same thing to the cafe on the corner or across the country. All by faith.

Virtually all of us, as we leave home to go to work, start our car without checking under the hood for a bomb. We also trust the brakes at each intersection and the driver of each oncoming car as we speed along the highway. We trust that no one will swerve into our path. Sometimes that trust is ill placed: someone, intoxicated, crashes into us. We are rushed to the hospital by an ambulance driver we never met and are attended by para-medics we don't know. We are injected with something we can't pronounce to produce an effect we don't understand. We are anesthetized by a total stranger, operated on by someone we never saw because we were under anesthesia when he began. We placed our life in the hands of total strangers!

How can all this be? Only by faith.

We put our money in the bank by faith and invest in the stock market by faith. Would anyone accuse Jay McCormick of biased, "religious" reporting when he headlined an article in the Money section of *USA Today* with the title, *"Investors Find Faith, Dow Up 29"*?[6] Of course not. We all live by faith each moment of every day. Those who do not are diagnosed (probably by a doctor they don't know) as paranoid.

Life would come to a virtual standstill should people stop living by faith. Unfortunately, many people think they *have* stopped, and they often resort to therapy in an effort to get their lives back together. Alan Loy McGinnis, author of *Bringing Out The Best In People,* expressed surprise that some therapists pay so little attention to belief systems. "I suppose they have been taught in graduate school to stay away from theological discussions, and they make the mistake of thinking that the good therapist spends the whole session talking about feelings and never discusses beliefs."[7]

When asked about their beliefs, many of McGinnis' patients say they are confused. "That's one reason I'm in therapy," they retort; *"I have no idea what I believe."* McGinnis tells of one such person who had come to view himself as an agnostic, confessing, "Everything seems so relative. Morals have all changed, standards have all changed, and I feel as if I'm doubting everything and believing nothing."

McGinnis advised him, "If you're not sure about certain religious beliefs, lay them aside for now, and concentrate on the things you're sure about." He asked the patient to make a list of those things he did believe in. A week later the man returned with a notepad full. The list went like this:[8]

* Animals deserve to be treated kindly.
* I'm happiest when I live near the ocean.
* Sex is great.
* It's important to tell the truth.
* Careful craftsmanship is always good and sloppy work always causes trouble.
* I love my kids more than anything.
* Hate is always wrong and love is always right.
* Kindness to someone in trouble is awfully admirable.

The patient discovered he actually did believe in something. "All people have belief systems," concluded McGinnis.[9] We can't live healthy, productive lives without them.

Dr. Norman Vincent Peale begins his book, *The Art of Real Happiness*, with this bold statement:

> Successful living hinges on the capacity to believe. The unconquerable of the world are those who have mastered the art of faith. They draw constantly on this inner source of strength, for they have acquired and hold ever fresh in their hearts an abiding faith in a Higher Power, and in their own destiny. Without such faith they are defenseless before the inevitable difficulties that all must face; with it they are armored against even the most cruel of adversaries.[10]

Interestingly, Jesus had much to say about faith and the role it plays in the lives of people. He spoke of faith as the most effective deterrent to fear:

"Don't be afraid; just believe," Jesus said to a man whose daughter was seriously ill (Mark 5:36).

In the midst of a storm he said to his disciples, "Why are you so afraid? Have you still no faith?" (Mark 4:40).

In his historic address on the Mount Jesus called his hearers away from anxiety to trust: "Therefore I tell you, do not worry about your life, what you will eat or drink; or about your body, what you will wear. Is not life more important than food, and the body more important than clothes? . . . Which of you by worrying can add a single hour to his life?" (Matt. 6:25, 27).

Jesus made enthusiastic claims regarding the practical power of faith: "I tell you the truth, if you have faith as small as a mustard seed, you can say to this mountain, 'Move from here to there,' and it will move. Nothing will be impossible to you" (Matt. 17:20). Mark records this statement in the positive, "Everything is possible for him who believes" (9:23).

No one knows the number of "mountains" which have been moved by faith. Insurmountable odds confront the human spirit at every bend in the road, rising up like Matterhorns defying anyone to conquer them. These mountains erect themselves in the areas of family, finance, friendships, jobs, recreation and wherever else people live. Either the mountains will overcome us, or our faith will overcome the mountains. This is the story of life.

James Whitcomb Brougher, Sr., commenting on the presence of faith in the field of science, affirmed, "There is not a scientific invention that has not had behind it the conviction in someone's soul that it could be done."[11] Among the many examples which he cited was Cyrus W. Field . . . "[who] became possessed with the conviction that a cable could be laid upon the bottom of the Atlantic Ocean and telegraphic communication could be established between Europe and America." The attempt failed time and time again. But he believed it could be done — he would not give up. His friends were disheartened, the public was skeptical, capitalists were unwilling to risk any more money; but Mr. Field organized a new company, made a new cable and finally laid it. The message was sent under the ocean, "Thank God, the cable is laid and is in perfect working order."[12]

Concluded Mr. Brougher, "When an idea grips a man with conviction, he ultimately will win." Randolph Miller concurs:

When a man's faith is the issue, he will fight with all his might. Under such pressures, a man either will break down or he will respond with a faith that gives meaning to all that he thinks and does. He has no time to become anxious, even though he may be afraid. . . . He develops maturity, poise, and judgment in the face of crisis. Nothing that life can do to him can sway him from his loyalty.[13]

An extreme and somewhat bizarre demonstration of the above statement is recorded in the *Reader's Digest* article entitled, "A Man Don't Know What He Can Do."[14] The article tells about a "giant" of a man who did what two wrecking trucks and a score of men could not do. He raised the crushed metal cab of a truck off its driver, tore out with his bare hands the brake pedal which had the driver's foot trapped and beat out the flames in the floor of the cab.

The "giant" was later discovered to be Charles Dennis Jones, an ordinary six foot two inch, 220 pound male. How did he do it? We may never fully understand, but fourteen months earlier his eight year old daughter had burned to death. Something kin to faith or conviction empowered Jones to accomplish the super-human feat at enormous risk. But as someone has said, "Faith is not believing something in spite of the evidence. It is the courage to do something in spite of the consequences." Nothing shall be impossible to him who believes.

* * * * * *

A young man walked into my office, extended his hand and said with great effort, "Hello, my name is David. I'm a representative for the Handicapped of America."

"You've come to the right place," I replied. "Everyone here is handicapped in one way or another. Tell me about yourself."

I listened to this bright young man tell his story. He was injured early in life and was left partially spastic. The mountains seemed insurmountable, yet he had risen to the top and was representing others who through faith were conquering mountains. Toward the close of his visit I asked him:

"What does the future hold for you?"

I shall never forget his answer. He looked me straight in the eye, straightened his shoulders and said, with some impediment but with determination and enthusiasm,

"I see no end to the possibilities!"

I could feel the mountains move. "All things are possible to him who believes."

* * * * * *

Hanging on our bedroom wall is a beautifully detailed drawing of a tree. The artist had signed it in the lower right hand corner, "Shelly Morgan." I first met Shelly in 1979 the day she walked with measured step into my office and told her story: She had been an active teenager but was diagnosed one day as having a brain tumor. She underwent surgery; a large tumor was removed, leaving her — so the doctors thought — more vegetable than human. She was completely paralyzed on her right side. The doctors told her parents to take her home and make her comfortable; that she wouldn't live long.

But she was determined to live, and live she did! Although the "mountains" were seemingly unsurmountable, she was determined. She was determined to walk again. She described her first step as "the hardest thing I ever did." After preparing herself by physical therapy for weeks, the day came for her to try to walk. Her father stood in front of her and invited her to come to him. She summoned all the strength of her impaired body, concentrated all her energy and took . . . one step and "fell into my father's arms, exhausted." And the mountains began to crumble.

After that, it was two steps; then three. Then five. She began to walk outside the house with a walker. Gradually she increased her distance until, on the day I met her, she reported she had walked that very day well over one thousand steps.

She began retraining herself to write and paint with her left hand. I asked her for one of her paintings, and she said she would send me one. Not long afterwards it arrived in the mail, and we proudly hung it in our home. On the back of the painting was a letter describing her continuing recovery and how she was involved more and more in abundant living. She closed by saying, "I'm keeping pretty busy painting, crocheting and exercising. Hope to see you again sometime. Love, Shelly."

And the mountains continued to move. "Nothing shall be impossible to him who believes."

*   *   *   *   *   *

At no time is faith more evident than in time of war. During World War II the churches and synagogues of England were filled with prayers. So were the foxholes on the battle fronts. Many a man has learned to pray in a foxhole. Faced with the prospect of death, something in us cries out for help. Call it what you will, faith is born in the foxholes of life. Even the atheist Robert Ingersall found words to express the stirring in his own heart as he stood by the grave of his brother:

"In the night of death, hope sees a star,
    And the listening love hears the rustle of a wing."

Norman Vincent Peale discovered through counseling hundreds of people that "everywhere you encounter people who are inwardly afraid, who shrink from life, who suffer from a deep sense of inadequacy and insecurity, who doubt their own powers. Deep within themselves they mistrust their ability to meet responsibilities or to grasp opportunities. Always they are beset by the vague and sinister fear that something is not going to be quite right. They do not believe that they have it in them to be what they want to be, and so they try to make themselves content with something less than that of which they are capable. Thousands upon thousands go crawling through life on their hands and knees, defeated and afraid."[15]

Has Peale reduced faith to a mere self-hypnosis or a pep talk which one administers to oneself apart from any deeper anchorings? Peale makes it clear in his preface to *The Power of Positive Thinking* that his approach to life is rooted deeply in faith. He says, "In formulating this simple philosophy I found my own answers in the teachings of Jesus Christ. I have merely tried to describe those truths in the language and thought forms understandable to present day people."[16]

Roland Hayes, the singer, passed on to Peale an interesting quote from his grandfather about faith:

"The trouble with lots of prayers," said the old man, "is they ain't got no suction."[17]

"Suction" was the elder Hayes' descriptive name for faith. It speaks volumes, doesn't it?

Then Peale advised, "Drive your prayers deep into your doubts, fears, inferiorities. Pray deep, big prayers that have plenty of suction and you will come up with powerful and vital faith."[18] I believe Jesus would have endorsed that.

Life Beyond the Present

On January 28, 1986, America sat in stunned silence as the ill-fated Challenger exploded shortly after lift off from Cape Canaveral. Seconds earlier the high expectations of the seven astronauts had been shared by all America and much of the world. Suddenly those expectations were blown out of the sky and sank to the floor of the Atlantic, unfulfilled. And America was left with two unanswered questions: "What went wrong?" and "Why did they launch in such cold weather?" Two other questions, whether voiced or not, would not go away: "What is the nature of man?" and "Is there anything beyond death?"

Some years ago a submarine sank off the coast of Massachusetts. The crew was still alive, but their oxygen supply was rapidly being depleted, and their radio could not send or receive. Divers were sent down to try to communicate with them. When communication had been established by a simple tapping on the skin of the sub, the crew sent the following message: "Is . . . there . . . any . . . hope?" In a sense, the crew of planet earth, as long as there has been life on earth, has been sending the same message: "Is there any hope?"

Jesus never used the word "hope" to address this seemingly universal longing of mankind. Yet one of the major themes of his teaching serves as the basis of all hope: "This life is not all there is to life." That this touches a responsive chord in most people is suggested by the fact that two books by actress Shirley McLain, *Out On A Limb* and *Dancing In The Light* have become best sellers totaling over 4 million copies. The underlying theme of both books is a westernized version of reincarnation, an alternative to the Christian doctrine of eternal life. The significant fact is that both books, along with other popular non-Christian philosophies, are proposing that humans do not cease to exist. And millions are receiving it warmly. There seems to be in humans an inbred desire to live on. The German philosopher Goethe attested that "it would be thoroughly impossible for a thinking being to think of a cessation of thought and life. Everyone carries the proof of immortality within himself, and quite involuntarily."[19]

Of course, there are those who disagree. Thomas H. Huxley, upon the death of his son, wrote a letter to his friend Charles Kingsley. Kingsley had written Huxley to comfort him by affirming the immortality of man. Huxley thanked him for writing, but said, among other things, "Nor does it help me to tell me that the aspirations of mankind — that my own highest aspirations even — lead me towards the doctrine of immortality. I doubt the fact, to begin with, but if it be so even, what is this but in grand words asking me to believe a thing because I like it?"[20]

And, strangely enough, some people live out a "death-wish" existence, and others commit suicide. But such human tragedy results more from despair than desire. Some end their life because they feel there is no hope, while others cling to life because they believe it is their only hope. Whatever the evidence, even paradoxical, it centers around the concepts of hope and life.

This longing is so universal that Carl Becker (1873-1945) tried to dismiss the "extraordinary sway" which the Christian story exercises over the minds of men by saying:

> No interpretation of the life of mankind ever more exactly reflected the experience, or effectively responded to the hopes of average men. . . . What could more adequately sum up the experience of the great majority? And what was the Christian story if not an application of this familiar individual experience to the life of mankind? Mankind had its youth, its happier time in the Garden of Eden, to look back upon, its present middle period of misfortunes to endure, its future security to hope for.[21]

Becker summed up the thought by saying, "The average man needed no theology to understand universal experience when presented in terms so familiar. . . ." Becker did not identify the "average man" about whom he spoke rather condescendingly, but his message comes through loud and clear: The average man is attracted to the concept that "this life is not all there is to this life."

Jesus answered the age old question, "Is there any hope?," with a resounding, "Yes." He insisted that there is much more to life than our present existence. He taught that we will live beyond the moment when our bodies finally are laid to rest, and that something very dramatic is going to happen to us at that point. Thus he advised:

"Do not work for food that spoils, but for food that endures to eternal life" (John 6:27).

"For whosever wants to save his life shall lose it, but whoever loses his life for me shall find it. What good will it be for a man if he gains the whole world, yet forfeits his soul? Or what can a man give in exchange for his soul?" (Matt. 16:25, 26).

"Do not store up for yourselves treasures on earth, where moth and rust destroy, and where thieves break in and steal. But store up for yourselves treasures in heaven, where moth and rust do not destroy, and where thieves do not break in and steal" (Matt. 6:19, 20).

That "this life is not all there is to life" is evident from Jesus' many teachings on final judgment. One statement captures the flavor of them all: "For the Son of Man is going to come in his Father's glory with his angels, and then he will reward each person according to what he has done" (Matt. 16:27). Commenting on how a final judgment appeals to the "average" man," Becker ovserved:

> . . . best of all — he [the average man] could understand that there should sometimes be an end made, a judgment pronounced upon the world of men and things, a day of reckoning in which evil men would be punished and good men rewarded: he could believe that with all his heart, with a conviction fortified by the stored-up memories of the injustices he had witnessed, and the unmerited injuries he had suffered. The average man could believe all that; and in the measure that he could believe it he could hope, he could so easily convince himself, that in that last day he would be found among those judged good, among those to be admitted into that other world in which things would be forever right.[22]

Becker was right. Jesus definitely touched a responsive chord when he spoke with confidence about life continuing beyond death: "Do not let your hearts be troubled. Trust in God; trust also in me. There are many rooms in my Father's house; otherwise I would have told you. I am going there to prepare a place for you. And if I go and prepare a place for you, I will come back and take you to be with me that you also may be where I am" (John 14:1-3).

Goethe seems to have been standing tiptoe on Jesus' shoulders when he said so adamantly: "It would be thoroughly impossible for a thinking being to think of a cessation of thought and life. Everyone carries the proof of immortality within himself, and quite involuntarily."

*   *   *   *   *   *

In the preceding material we have considered five major areas of Jesus' teachings. Do they have the ring of truth about them? Each of us must answer for himself. Though you may not yet have the ultimate answer regarding Jesus' identity, perhaps by now you are beginning to understand why Jesus has had such an impact on human life.

We turn now to the most obvious of all Jesus' teachings: his philosophy of love.

1. Bill Glasgall, "On the Cheap: The Unhappy Life of J. Paul Getty," *Business Week,* 21 April 1986, p. 10.

2. For an excellent extended study of this philosophy see Gayle Erwin, *The Jesus Style* (Waco, TX: Word Publishers, 1986).

3. Mark Hatfield, *Between a Rock and a Hard Place* (Waco, TX: Word Books, 1976), p. 26.

4. Marian Christi, "Leo Buscaglia: 'Dr. Hug'," *Boston Globe,* Oct. 21, 1984, Sec. B, pp. 15, 19.

5. From *Bulletin,* King of Prussia, PA, Church of Christ.

6. Jay McCormick, "Investors Find Faith, Dow Up 29," *USA Today,* 28 May 1986, Sec. B, p. 1.

7. Alan Loy McGinnis, *Bringing Out The Best in People* (Minneapolis: Augsburg Publishing House, 1985), pp. 45, 46.

8. Ibid., p. 47.

9. Ibid.

10. Norman Vincent Peale, *The Art of Real Happiness* (New York: Prentice Hall, Inc., 1950), p. 3.

11. James Whitcomb Brougher, *Life and Laughter* (Valley Forge: The Judson Press, 1950), p. 28.

12. Ibid., p. 30.

13. Randolph Crump Miller, *Living With Anxiety* (Philadelphia: Pilgrim Press, 1971), p. 105.

14. *Reader's Digest*, October, 1952.

15. Norman Vincent Peale, *The Power of Positive Thinking* (Greenwich, Conn.: Fawcett Publications, 1952), p. 20. Maxwell Maltz, M.D., concurs. See his book, *Psycho-Cybernetics* (New York: Pocket Books/Simon and Schuster, Inc., 1960), pp. ix, 4.

16. Peale, Op. cit., *Power*, p. vii.

17. Peale, Op. cit., *Power*, p. 18.

18. Ibid.

19. Goethe, *On Immortality*, as quoted in *The Practical Cogitator*, eds. Charles P. Curtis, Jr. and Ferris Greenslet (Boston: Houghton Mifflin Company, 1945), p. 510. Goethe's passing observation has been scientifically documented by authors such as Elisabeth Kubler-Ross, *On Death and Dying* (New York: Macmillan Publishing Co., 1969).

20. T. H. Huxley, "Letter to Kingsley," as quoted in *The Practical Cogitator*, eds. Charles P. Curtis, Jr. and Ferris Greenslet (Boston: Houghton Mifflin Company, 1945), p. 515.

21. Carl L. Becker, "The Last Judgment," as quoted in *The Practical Cogitator*, eds. Charles P. Curtis, Jr. and Ferris Greenslet (Boston: Houghton Mifflin Company, 1945), p. 509.

22. Ibid., p. 510.

7

Imposing Philosophy

"Man's greatest dignity, his most essential and peculiar power, the most intimate secret of his humanity is his capacity to love."[1]

And yet:

"Love" is so loosely used that we probably should declare a moratorium on it. When you can "love" an Oscar Mayer wiener and God in the same breath, you have to wonder what the word does mean.[2]

*   *   *   *   *   *

Leo Buscaglia, modern day apostle of love known as "Dr. Hug," once learned that one of his love books had been spotted in a Manhattan pornography shop. "That's good," responded Buscaglia, "because anybody looking for a pornographic book is badly in need of love."[3]

A pornography shop is a far cry from the kind of context in which Jesus would have set his teaching on love. Or is it? Did not Jesus often associate with and teach disreputables? Jesus was known as the "Dr. Hug" of his day — a "friend of tax collectors and sinners" (Luke 7:34).

When Buscaglia, professor at the University of Southern California, announced he would start a class on "love" they laughed at him. Says Buscaglia, "Colleagues snickered hah-

hah-hah and said: 'O, so you're teaching a *love* class to all those pretty young things. Hah-Hah!' " His colleagues were equating love with sex. But Buscaglia made a clear distinction: "What I wanted to teach people is to be able to live joyfully with one another."[4]

Setting aside momentarily Jesus' teaching on love, we will attempt to determine how central love is to the pursuit of life and happiness. Whatever we may identify as love — whether affirmation or charity or sex or friendship; motherly love, fatherly love, or brotherly love — we all know we do not fare well without it.

That which is most often equated with love is sex. One need only listen to the popular songs on the current "Top Forty" or the Country & Western favorites to understand that love is equated with sex and is #1 on all the charts. Sex occupies a large place in human consciousness. And it goes without saying that the human race could not continue without the sexual act that reproduces life. Nor could any life form, animal or plant, continue without the sex act which reproduces it. Love, therefore, in the biological sense, sits right at the center of all physical life.

But there is much more to love than the sex act — even among the lower animals. In *The Friendship Factor,* author McGinnis observes, "The young of all mammals snuggle and cuddle against the body of their mother and against the body of their siblings. Almost every animal enjoys being stroked or otherwise having its skin pleasurably stimulated. Dogs appear to be insatiable in their appetite for petting, cats will purr for it, and dolphins love to be gently stroked."[5]

And no one yet has plumbed the depth of human dependency on love. We soon discover "a thousand kingdoms that at first overwhelm us by their variety and number. Here is a couple walking arm in arm in ecstasy; this, certainly, is the way of lovers and, presumably, a loving state of soul. But here is a mother cradling her child, and this, too, is love. And there is a youth leading his little brother; and this, too, is love. The handclasp I exchanged with my friend, the coin I drop in the blind man's cup, the bittersweet generosity of hidden self-sacrifice . . . what a multitude of forms love takes! Protective strength and timid sensitivity, the frank exchange of a common gift, the tears that beg pardon and the ones that forgive, the visit to the sick man, Mermione's wrath and Abraham's poised blade — only one thing is common to them all: the love that evoked them."[6]

*   *   *   *   *   *

The babies in the South American foundling home were dying, and the doctors could not determine the cause. The children showed no signs of disease, conditions were sanitary, and the food was good. But for some strange reason the babies lost interest in their food and toys. They grew weaker and died. Dr. Rene Spitz tells the pitiful, revealing story:

A team of doctors from the United Nations was summoned to observe and diagnose the situation. After a few days of observation, the U.N. doctors prescribed this strange remedy: "For ten minutes of every waking hour, each child is to be picked up, hugged and kissed, petted and played with, then hugged and kissed some more." Within a short time the symptoms disappeared, and the epidemic subsided. The children began to eat again and play with their toys. And when their ten minutes came they were waiting with outstretched arms. And so the mysterious malady was arrested, but not before it had taken the life of thirty-four of the babies and had left another twenty-one hopelessly neurotic. The illness is called "marasmus" (a Greek word meaning "wasting away"), a mysterious emaciation of the body, which seems to strike the very young and the very old when those in between do not show them enough love.[7]

But what is true of babies is true also of adults. "Love — love of people and love of his audiences," says Bob Hope's wife Dolores, "is what keeps 83 year old Bob young. . . . The big thing is love. The more love you have, the more you communicate it and the more it comes back to you."[8] Erich Fromm maintains that "the deepest need of man . . . is the need to overcome his separateness, to leave the prison of his aloneness, and that the absolute failure to achieve this means insanity."[9] Fromm affirms that unless the deepest need is fulfilled, insanity is the result. How does he suggest this need be met?

By love. "Love is the only way of knowledge, which in the act of union answers my quest. In the act of loving, of giving myself, in the act of penetrating the other person, I find myself, I discover myself, I discover us both, I discover man."[10]

Fromm continues to speak in absolute terms when he says, "The only way of full knowledge lies in the act of love: this act transcends thought, it transcends words. It is the daring plunge into the experience of union."[11] Though he speaks eventually of biological union, initially he addresses the "universal, existential need for union." Only after affirming the general, universal need does he proceed to speak of the more specific biological need — the union between male and female.[12] But in regard to both, Fromm calls love "the only way . . .," thus affirming love's unique centrality to human existence and sanity. As a psychologist he goes so far as to say, "the ultimate consequence of psychology is love."[13]

"Thresholds," a remarkable new approach to the rehabilitation of schizophrenics, has effectively demonstrated Fromm's thesis. John G. Hubbell entitles his review of the new program: "Thresholds: A Way Out of Madness."[14] He describes the program as "a unique blend of medication, counseling, work opportunities and love [which] is returning the mentally ill to active meaningful lives."

Bruce Larson, in his book, *The Relational Revolution*,[15] makes some interesting observations on "the growing suspicions about the effectiveness of psychiatry and psychotherapy" and, contrastingly, the amazing results of non-professional small groups such as Alcoholics Anonymous. He asks the question, "What are those factors [in the non-professional therapy] that seem to bring healing or help to persons with problems?" His answer: "First, the people in the group dared to get involved."[16] This "daring to get involved" with another person is what Fromm called "penetration" or "the act of love."[17]

Larson also tells of a conversation he had with Dr. Paul Tournier, one of the best-known counselors and therapists of our time. In the conversation, Dr. Tournier confessed, "I am very embarrassed by all these people who come to see me. I don't know how to help people. I don't do anything at all.

What is important is that people try to find their way and that I try to understand and support them, to welcome them. What is important is that people find me a true friend, someone in whom they can confide everything."[18] Larson, then, observed: "Dr. Tournier is not describing a professional relationship but one of love and trust and empathy."[19]

"This Medicine, Love" is the title of the first chapter of Dr. Karl Menninger's book, *Love Against Hate*. In commenting on Freud's theory that 'the impulse to live and love is an instinctual endowment of human beings and a source of strength in opposition to self-destructiveness,' Menninger observed succinctly, "Die we must, ultimately, but in the meantime we can live if we can love."[20] Consequently, says Robert E. Fitch, "There is a choice that every man must make. It is the choice to love or hate . . . this first choice must be made. . . . To seek to evade it . . . is to destroy the self. . . . For to be afraid to love is the greatest cowardice that can befall a man."[21]

The above statements by psychiatrists and psychologists are part of the mounting evidence regarding the place love occupies in the healthy human psyche. Such testimony provides a scientific explanation for love being the common thread running through the great world religions. Harvard University's Pitirim A. Sorokin observed that "all great apostles of love and moral educators of humanity themselves have been filled with love, generously granted it to anyone, and endeavored to increase and to improve the production of love." Sorokin listed Christ, Buddha, St. Francis of Assisi, Gandhi and many smaller producers of love, such as "kind and good neighbors, and all who habitually perform unselfish acts of love."[22]

When we probe the "gulf-stream of religious thought and experience . . . as human history has gone steadily on . . . we find substantial agreement in regard to these matters among those whose lives and testimonies have affected the world most deeply."[23] Reaching far back into time, one comes to the Great Empire of Egypt (1600 B.C.-525 B.C.) and to the first great religious leader of whom we have any record outside the biblical history: Amen-Hotep IV (ca. 1380 B.C.). Prof. Horne describes him as "the last sovereign of the mighty Eighteenth Dynasty [and] kingly advocate of the new idea [monotheism]."[24] In his enthusiasm for the god he called Aton, Amen-

Hotep even changed his ownname to Iknu-Aton ("worshipper of Aton"). Unlike the angry, wrathful gods of the heathen pantheon, Aton, the creator God, was a god of love and mercy,

> Who hears the prayer of him who is in captivity,
> Who is kindly of heart when one calls on him,
> Who saves the timid from the haughty,
> Who separates the weak from the strong,
> Lord of knowledge, in whose mouth is Taste;
> For love of whom the Nile comes,
> Lord of sweetness, great in love,
> At whose coming the people live.[25]

Aton sounds much like Jehovah, the God revealed to the Hebrew nation approximately the same time but in much greater detail and clarity. According to Exodus 34:6-7 Jehovah described himself to Moses as:

> Jehovah, Jehovah, a God merciful and gracious, slow to anger, and abounding in steadfast love and faithfulness, keeping steadfast love for thousands, forgiving iniquity and transgression and sin, but who will by no means clear the guilty, visiting the iniquity of the fathers upon the children and the children's children, to the third and fourth generation.

Not only was love identified as the principal character of Jehovah, it was isolated as the basic response Jehovah seeks from those who worship him. To this day, the Jew considers the Shemah the foundation stone of his religion: "Hear, O Israel: The Lord our God is one Lord; And you shall love the Lord your God with all your heart, and with all your soul, and with all your might" (Deut. 6:4, 5). The detailed revelation of Jehovah to the Israelite nation as a God of love and mercy finds no parallel in history.

But though there is no parallel, there is almost universal corroboration. We find an excellent example in Zoroaster, who lived some seven hundred fifty years after Moses. "The Ancient Sage," as the Greeks called him, was "the first known teacher of the Aryan race."[26] One quotation from later Zoroastrian writings reveals what was central to their religion:

> To enjoy the benefits of providence is wisdom; to enable others to enjoy them is virtue. He who is indifferent to the welfare of others does not deserve to be called a man. . . . He needs no other rosary

whose life is strung with beads of loving thought. . . . Diversity of
worship has divided the race into countless nations; from all their
dogmas we may select one: Divine love . . .[27]

Confucius concurred with this and, though he framed his
philosophy in the negative, he willed good for one's neighbor
by the principle of reciprocity: "Do not do unto others what
you would not want done to yourself."[28]

There was another great Chinese teacher by the name of
Mohti, a younger contemporary of Confucius. His religion, according to a zealous critic, was wholly that of love. Said
Mencius of Mohti: "Mohti loved all men and would gladly
wear out his whole being from head to heel for the benefit of
mankind."[29] The doctrine which lay at the heart of such
conduct is clearly expressed in the following: "Love is at the
heart of all things, and the way of salvation for the world is
therefore to practice love, whether in private or public life.
Where there is mutual love there is peace; where there is
mutual hatred there is war."[30]

Next among the oriental sages who made a significant
impact on the world was Guatama Buddha. Prof. Horne maintains that: "For our Western world the Buddhist faith and the
Buddhist literature hold a more living interest than any other
of the books or teachings of the Far East . . . both in its doc-
trines and in its history, [Buddhism] bears a striking resem-
blance to Christianity."[31]

Though there are many differences, one of the similarities
Prof. Horne points out is the insistence of both religions on
kindliness toward every living thing: "A Buddhist monk will
not even kill an insect that annoys him, but will gently remove
it from his person. This universal kindness differs from the
Christian teaching of universal love only by its lack of warmth.
Love is too intense a feeling to accompany the Buddhist doctrine of the suppression of human passions."[32]

But since the love which Jesus enjoined is not a feeling but
a decision, there is a similarity between it and the kindliness
encouraged by Buddha. It is graphically described in verse
that has been called the "Buddhist Thirteenth Chapter of First
Corinthians":

Just as with her own life a mother shields from hurt
      her own, her only, child —
let all-embracing thoughts (of love)
      for all that lives be thine.

—an all-embracing love for all the universe
      in all its heights and depths and breadth,
unstinted love, unmarred by hate within,
      not rousing enmity.

So, as you stand or walk, or sit, or lie,
      reflect with all your might on this;
—'tis deemed a state divine.[33]

A follower of Buddha summed it up in these words, "loving deeds, loving word and loving hearts . . . all the other means that can be used toward doing right avail not the sixteenth part of the emancipation through love."[34]

A single example of Buddha's influence is that recorded in the life of the great King Asoka. H. G. Wells numbers him among the first six great benefactors of the human race and says of him:

> Among the tens of thousands of names of monarchs that crowd the columns of history, their majesties and graciousnesses and serenities and royal highnesses and the like, the name of Asoka shines, and shines almost alone, a star. . . . More living men cherish his memory today than have ever heard the names of Constantine or Charlemagne.[35]

King Asoka left behind some thirty carved inscriptions which tell of his conquests, his life and devotion to Buddhism. Prof. Horne, in his Introduction to the Edicts of Asoka, simply reports that after several years of military conquest, Asoka became convinced, about 354 B.C., that he could best extend and consolidate his domains by ruling over the hearts of men. "He had already accepted Buddhism for himself," wrote Prof. Horne, "and he now began to make every effort to spread it over the world by peaceful means."[36]

But Williams, in his colorful account, supplies graphic details. He informs us that "In the ninth year of Asoka's reign, he coveted the territory of a nearby people called the Kalingas and waged a cruel war of conquest against them killing one hundred thousand, taking another one hundred thousand captive and leaving behind him many thousands maimed and wounded. After it was all over, the brutalities and sufferings which he had so selfishly inflicted upon a helpless people weighed so heavily upon his conscience that when the teachings of Buddha on the sacredness of life were brought to his attention, such was his penitence that he vowed then and there never again to wage war or resort to any form of violence in extending or even preserving the domain of empire."[37] Asoka gave himself the name "Piyadasi," which means "The Benevolent One."[38] Thus one of the tyrants of history became one of its benefactors through the power of love.

As Olds observes, "Zoroaster, Confucius, Lao-tze, Mohti, Buddha, Socrates, and the great prophets of Israel and Judah — did there ever come to birth at any time, either before or since, in one continent and in a single period in the world's history, such a galaxy of stars as that to which the world even yet turns for light?"[39] They all, with one voice, affirm love to be the center of the universe.

There is one exception to this otherwise universal rule: Mohammedanism. That there should be any exception at all is puzzling until it is recognized that Islam (Mohammedanism) did not originate as a search for God but as an aberrant attempt to unify the divided Arab tribes under one banner and spill over into the surrounding nations. The method employed was force. The bloodshed that Islam has left in its wake, from Mohammed to the present, requires that Islam be placed in a category different from the great world religions under discussion. T. P. Hughes confirms such a judgment:

> Notwithstanding its fair show of outward observances, and its severe legal enactments, there is something in Islam which strikes at the very root of morals, poisons domestic life, and in its truest sense, disorganizes society. Freedom of judgment is crushed, and a barrier has been raised not merely against the advance of Christianity, but against the progress of civilization itself. For everything in religion, in law, in life, and in thought, has been measured for all time. Mohammedanism admits of no progress in morals, law or commerce. It fails to regenerate the man, and it is equally powerless in regenerating the nation.[40]

What an indictment! And the bloodbath Islam continues to bring upon the world confirms it. That which is lacking in Islam which sets it apart, tragically, from all the world is its lack of focus on love.

But what about the non-religious? What importance do they place on love? First, it should be understood that there are no non-religious persons. All humans are religious — incurably religious. Even those who affirm they are non-religious must admit that, though they may be non-Christian, or non-Jewish, or non-Buddhist, they have their own religion, and it guides their life, for good or ill.

But, aside from that, it may have some bearing on our question regarding the appropriateness of Jesus' teaching about love if we can call as a witness someone who has set himself as an avowed enemy of Christianity. The one who comes most readily to my mind is the philosopher Bertrand Russell. In his little booklet, "Why I Am Not A Christian," he sets out to explain why he does not believe in God and why he does not accept the claims of Christ. But in the midst of all his reasoning, there jumps out at the reader a chapter entitled, "What I Believe." It was interesting to see in the middle of that chapter a section entitled, "The Good Life." Set apart in italics was the heading: *The good life is one inspired by love and guided by knowledge.* This noble description of the good life holds love as the foundation: "Although both love and knowledge are necessary, love is in a sense more fundamental, since it will lead intelligent people to seek knowledge, in order to find out how to benefit those whom they love."[41] This comes pretty close to Jesus' definition of love.

But Russell was even more emphatic about the need for love in human life. Dr. Stanley L. Jaki comments on philosopher Russell's speech at Columbia University in 1950:

> When Bertrand Russell stated . . . that Christian love or compassion was the thing most needed by modern humans, he moved revealingly close to declaring intellectual bankruptcy on his and many others' behalf. He said much more about Christian love. Although fully familiar with the enormous power of modern science, medicine and technology, he held high Christian love as the *answer* to human needs in the broadest sense: "If you have Christian love," [Russell] declared to a stunned audience, "you have motive for existence, a guide for action, a reason for courage, an imperative for intellectual honesty."[42]

In view of the dominant, central place love occupies in religion, literature, music, stage, art and science (both psychological and physiological) it is not surprising that love was that very essence of Jesus' philosophy. Love did not fit into Jesus' philosophy: love *was* his philosophy. When asked by the legal experts what was the most important command in the Law of Moses, Jesus promptly replied:

> "Love the Lord your God with all your heart, with all your soul and with all your mind." This is the first and greatest commandment. And the second is like it: "Love your neighbor as yourself." All the Law and the Prophets hang on these two commandments (Matt. 22: 35-40).

Jesus thus affirmed that everything in religion and life finds its point of reference in love for God (v. 37), love for self (v. 39a) and love for neighbor (v. 39b). This was his philosophy.

But the most unique application of love, and the one for which Jesus is most noted, is his command to "Love your enemies, do good to those who hate you, bless those who curse you, pray for those who mistreat you" (Luke 6:27-28). His own countrymen had been trained in the tradition, "Hate your enemy" (Matt. 5:43). So when Jesus came saying, "Love your enemy," he caused quite a stir. He went on to say, "If you love only those who love you, what reward will you get? . . . And if you greet only your brothers, what are you doing more than others? Do not even pagans do that?" (Matt. 5:46-48). Thus he called his disciples to the highest, most difficult demonstration of love — love of enemies.

Was Jesus right in his emphasis on love? Is love the most important quality in life? Is love for one's enemies a desirable trait? Or is such a philosophy purely an idealistic dream with little or no basis in reality? We have seen that, almost without exception, the great people and the great religions of the world concur with Jesus that love is indeed the center and heart of the universe. Leo Buscaglia, in his book, *Personhood,* sums up a survey of the world religions by saying,

> . . . there is little dissonance among the several philosophical and religious systems in their suggestion as to what it means to live in full humanness . . . the way of the fully functioning person is clear. . . . The overall, overriding code seems to arise from what has been scoffed at as a supreme and simplistic platitude, "Do unto others as you would have them do unto you."[43]

When we stop and ponder the hunger for love which we experience moment by moment, day by day, throughout the nights and over the years with seemingly no cessation, with all the others who throughout the ages have pointed unanimously to love as the center of human existence, we know that love is indeed the heart of the universe. Jesus was right.

---

1. Thomas Merton, *The Power and Meaning of Love* (New York: Farrar, Straus & Cudahy, 1980), p. 98.

2. Dan Anders, "Profile of a Christian," *We Preach Christ Crucified*, ed. Dr. Jerry Rushford (Malibu, CA: Pepperding University Press, 1986), p. 93.

3. Christi, Op. cit.

4. Ibid.

5. McGinnis, Op. cit., pp. 85, 86.

6. Maurice Nedoncelle, *Love and the Person*, trans. Sr. Ruth Adelaide, S. C. (New York: Sheed and Ward, 1966), p. 6.

7. Rene A. Spitz, "Hospitalism: An Inquiry Into the Genesis of Psychiatric Conditions in Early Childhood" in R. S. Eissler et al. (eds.), *Psychoanalytic Study of the Child*, Vol. 1 (New York: International Universities Press, 1945), pp. 53-73; and "Hospitalism: A Follow-up Report," *Psychoanalytic Study of the Child*, Vol. 2 (New York: International Universities Press, 1946).

8. *Globe Magazine*, July 1, 1986, p. 24.

9. Erich Fromm, *The Art of Loving* (New York: Bantam Books, 1956), p. 8.

10. Ibid., p. 26.

11. Ibid.

12. Ibid., p. 27.

13. Ibid.

14. John G. Hubbell, *Reader's Digest*, August, 1986, p. 37.

15. Bruce Larson, *The Relational Revolution* (Waco, TX: Word Books, 1976), pp. 111-117.

16. Ibid., p. 113.

17. Fromm. Op. cit., p. 26.

18. Ibid., p. 116.

19. Ibid.

20. Karl Menninger, *Love Against Hate* (New York: Harcourt, Brace & World, Inc., 1942), p. 5.

21. Robert E. Fitch, *Of Love and Suffering* (Philadelphia: The Westminster Press, n.d.), p. 15.

22. Pitirim A. Sorokin, "Love, Its Aspects," *Explorations of Altruistic Love and Behavior*, A Symposium edited by Pitirim A. Sorokin (Boston: Beacon Press, 1950), p. 62.

23. Charles Burnell Olds, *Love: The Issue* (Boston: The Christopher Publishing House, n.d.), p. 33.

24. See "Hymns To The One Universal God," *The Sacred Books and Literature of the East*, Vol. 2 of 14 vols., ed. Charles F. Horne (New York: Parke, Austin, and Lipscomb, Inc., 1917), p. 290.

25. Ibid., p. 298.

26. Op. cit., *Sacred Books of the East*, vol. 7, p. 1.

27. David Rhys Williams, *World Religions and the Hope for Peace* (Boston: The Beacon Press, 1951), p. 70. See also *Sacred Books and Early Literature of Ancient Persia*, Vol. 7 of 14 vols. *Sacred Books and Early Literature of the East*, ed. Charles F. Horne (New York: Parke, Austin, and Lipscomb, Inc., 1917).

28. Williams, Op. cit., p. 9.

29. Harry Kingman, "Mohti, One of the Immortals," *Unity:* Vol. XCIX, No. 20 (August 22, 1927), pp. 331, 332.

30. Ibid.

31. See *The Sacred Books and Early Literature of the East*, Vol. 10: *India and Buddhism*, ed. Prof. Charles F. Horne (New York: Parke, Austin, and Lipscomb, 1917), p. 3.

32. Ibid., p. 7.

33. *The Teachings of the Compassionate Buddha*, ed. E. A. Burtt (New York: Mentor Books, 1955), p. 47.

34. Ibid., p. 50.

35. H. G. Wells, Op. cit., Vol. I, pp. 432, 433.

36. See "Edicts of Asoka," *Sacred Book and Early Literature of Buddhism*, Vol. 10 of *Sacred Books and Early Literature of the East*, ed. Charles F. Horne, 14 Vols. (New York: Parke, Austin, and Lipscomb, Inc., 1917), p. 15.

37. Williams, Op. cit., pp. 62, 63.

38. Ibid., p. 14.

39. Olds, Op. cit., p. 39.

40. T. P. Hughes, as quoted by Frank Ballard, *The Miracles of Unbelief* (Edinburg: T. & T. Clark, 1900), p. 290.

41. Bertrand Russell, *Why I Am Not A Christian* and Other Essays, ed. Paul Edwards (London: George Allen & Unwin Ltd., 1957), pp. 44, 45.

42. Stanley L. Jaki, "Science: From the Womb of Religion," *The Christian Century* (Oct. 7, 1987), p. 851.

43. Leo F. Buscaglia, *Personhood* (New York: Fawcett Columbine, 1978), p. 89.

8

Impelling Relationships

I once read a story about a colony of ants who over the years had developed a strange aberration in their walk. It had evolved into a "one-two-three-skip" gait. This peculiar mutation hindered them in both work and play, but they didn't know any different. As far as they knew, they all were perfectly normal.

One-two-three-skip!

One-two-three-skip!

Then one day there appeared among them an ant who did not walk like they did. He walked with a smooth one-two-three-four gait. He was a strange sight. At first the other ants were curious; then they were furious.

"How dare he walk differently from us!"

And they killed him.

* * * * * *

I wonder if this is what happened to Jesus. According to every record, biblical and non-biblical, his life was different from those around him; so different that, though at first his contemporaries were curious, finally in fury they killed him. Jesus was too different to be tolerated.

But how was he different? As far as his contemporaries were concerned, Jesus was one of them — a boy who grew up on their street, played with their children, made annual pilgrimages to Jerusalem along with the rest of them, and on one occasion got lost as children sometimes do. Jesus was a man who "came to his own." His neighbors recognized him as one of themselves: "Isn't this the carpenter? Isn't this Mary's son and the brother of James, Joses, Judas and Simon? Aren't his sisters here with us?" they asked (Mark 6:3). So, evidently, Jesus did not stand out as different in this basic respect.

Also, Jesus was not considered different due to his revealing some strange new theory unrelated, or contradictory, to life as people knew life ought to be lived. In fact, what he taught struck all too close to home. He taught with an authority his countrymen recognized (Matt. 7:28, 29). They identified his teachings precisely as "wisdom": "Where did this man get all this . . . wisdom?" they asked (Mark 6:2). So Jesus' ethic struck a responsive chord among his own people. And beyond his own people. His philosophy of love, we have noticed, has met with virtually unanimous agreement from the founders of world religions and leaders in philosophy and psychology. Even those antagonistic to institutional Christianity concur with the heart of Jesus' teaching. Jesus did not introduce a controversial, new ethic, but only what had been universally recognized as right and good and true.

This broad consensus, in addition to lending considerable weight to Jesus' claims, also puts his teachings in proper perspective. For the most part Jesus did not claim that his teachings were novel or original. He claimed only that they were true. The fact that so many great thinkers and leaders of history concur with him shows something of how close to the heart Jesus struck.

You may be asking, "What difference does it make?" Just this: It was precisely people's knowledge of what was right and true and good to which Jesus appealed as he presented his kingdom-of-heaven teachings. His basic teaching tool — the parable — assumes this. He told stories his hearers knew to be true to life and then "threw along besides" those truths (which is the meaning of "parable") the spiritual application to which he called his hearers.

He also solicited input from his hearers. One day when a lawyer asked him what he should do to inherit eternal life Jesus replied, "What is written in the Law? How do you read?" Upon hearing the answer Jesus said, "You have answered correctly; do this and you will live" (Luke 10:25-28). Thus Jesus appealed to the conscience of the people to verify his teachings.

Then, in what way was Jesus different from those around him and from those who came after him? The most obvious quality Jesus possessed seems to have been a consistent embodiment of all those traits people already knew to be right and good and true — including the basic human longing for immortality. As Hans Heinrich Wendt says, "The whole of the active work of Jesus was an exposition of his teaching with his own example."[1] Perfect equivalency between founder and ethic is unique to Christianity. Professor H. H. Henson observes that there is no other religion in which its historic founder is recognized as "a norm of personal morality. . . . Jesus alone is able to offer himself as the sufficient illustration of his own doctrine."[2]

If one were called upon to identify the one, constant, permeating quality of Jesus' life which entitles it to be called original or unique, it is the quality of consistency. He was uniquely consistent in everything he did and said. His teachings were consistent, his actions were consistent, and his actions and his teachings were consistent with each other. This much his adversaries knew. And it was precisely at this point that they directed their attacks. The many hypothetical and real life situations they presented to Jesus had this underlying hope: prove Jesus inconsistent. So, "When Jesus left there, the Pharisees and the teachers of the Law began to oppose him fiercely and to besiege him with questions, waiting to catch him in something he might say" (Luke 11:53, 54). The records show that his adversaries were never able to prove him inconsistent.

But there were two other dimensions of consistency which loomed large in Jesus' life: 1) his actions and his teachings were consistent with the ultimate life situation to which he had dedicated himself, and 2) his actions and his teachings were consistent with the immediate needs of the individuals whose paths he crossed along the way. Consistency in these two dimensions is extremely significant as one attempts to assess the life of Jesus, and it is this which occupies the remainder of this chapter.

In regard to the first quality, author Adrian Van Kaam, in his book *Religion and Personality* identifies consistency as one of the traits of the mature, "integrated" personality. Since "man as existence always finds himself in meaningful surroundings," Van Kaam asks, "in what way does a real personality relate himself to the life situation?" The author then affirms that "one of the dominant characteristics of [a real personality] is stability and quiet consistency."[3]

> . . . The mature personality has found his position in relation to both himself and to the world. He has taken his stand, and this decision consistently colors his attitudes toward everything that happens to him . . . the basic decisions which the [mature] personality has made render him sure and calm on all occasions. . . . He remains himself in spite of turbulence and disturbance.[4]

If any single quality in the life of Jesus stands out boldly, it is this: he was unreservedly committed to doing the will of God. From the very earliest incident in his adolescence in which Jesus affirmed quite resolutely, "Didn't you know I had to be in my Father's house?" (Luke 2:49), to his last moments in which he cried, "It is finished . . . Father, into your hands I commit my spirit" (John 19:30; Luke 23:46), the set of his mind is obvious. He saw clearly what the will of God called him to do and to suffer, and nothing could dissuade him — not the temptation at the beginning of his ministry to receive "all the kingdoms of the world" through an alliance with Satan (Matt. 4:8-10), nor Peter's insistence that it was not necessary for Jesus to die (Matt. 16:22, 23), nor the messianic enthusiasm which caused the mob to attempt to make him king by force (John 6:15).

Jesus resolutely "set his face toward Jerusalem" (Luke 9:53, RSV) and taught his disciples repeatedly that he "must go to Jerusalem and suffer many things from the elders and chief priests and scribes, and be killed, and on the third day be raised" (Matt. 16:21). Nothing could change his mind, though at times the prospect of his death all but paralyzed him: "I have a baptism to undergo, and how distressed I am until it is completed!'' (Luke 12:50). On one occasion as they were going up to Jerusalem, Jesus was so obsessed with the thought of his death that he was walking ahead of his disciples, evidently, in a way that was not characteristic of him; "and the disciples were astonished, and those who followed were afraid" (Mark 10:32). He turned and explained that it was his preoccupation with his impending death that was causing him to act that way (10:33, 34).

The day before his death Jesus seems to have been overwhelmed by the thought of his impending death, answering questions that were not being asked (John 12:20-23), and talking, it seems, to himself, reassuring himself that "unless a kernal of wheat falls to the ground and dies, it remains only a single seed. But if it dies, it produces many seeds" (v. 24); and that "he who loves his life will lose it, while the man who hates his life in this world will keep it for eternal life" (v. 25). He asked and answered his own questions: "Now my heart is troubled. And what shall I say, 'Father, save me from this hour?' No. It was for this very reason I came to this hour" (John 12:27). In spite of the noble answer Jesus gave himself, John records that Jesus "departed and hid himself . . ." (v. 30). Later in the day he reappeared (v. 44), resolved to fulfill what he knew to be his destiny.

He definitely was not an emotionless robot. The last night of his life found him in the garden of Gethsemane, saying to his disciples, "My soul is overwhelmed with sorrow to the point of death" . . . and going a little farther he fell with his face to the ground and prayed, "My Father, if it is possible, may this cup be taken from me. Yet not as I will, but as you will" (Matt. 26:38, 39). He made the request three times. And Luke records that Jesus' sweat fell to the ground "like drops of blood" (22:44).

Moments later, however, Jesus returned to his sleeping disciples to announce that his captors had arrived. Who can fail to be impressed with the calmness with which he received his captors, and the quiet dignity he displayed before the Jewish and Roman courts. He knew his hour had come; that he had been born for that very moment (John 18:37).

Jesus' uncompromising commitment to what he perceived as his ultimate purpose is clearly seen in a statement he made the night of his arrest: "It is written, 'And he was numbered with the transgressors'; and I tell you that this must be fulfilled in me. Yes, what is written about me is reaching its fulfillment" (Luke 22:37). Here Jesus clearly and intentionally identifies himself with the suffering servant of Isaiah 53. He was so bold as to say, "What is written about *me* has its fulfillment." Thus we see how deeply rooted in Jesus was the consciousness of his destiny, and how committed he was to its fulfillment: "This scripture *must* be fulfilled in me."

So clearly does this motif of suffering and death show through the records that Dr. Hugh Schonfield, in *The Passover Plot,* charged Jesus himself with being the "comprehensive engineer" of his own execution.

> Jesus, knowing full well what he was doing, had quite deliberately forced [the council] . . . by his skilfully planned and calculated activities. . . . He had himself made doubly sure that they would proceed to extremes against him by goading them with his words and behavior, so that any possible mitigation of their severity would be offset by the personal animus he had intentionally created.[5]

Schonfield provided no category which would allow Jesus both foreknowledge of his death and authentic identity as Messiah. But one thing Schonfield could not deny: the consistency of Jesus' life, even in the midst of his impending death.

But there was a second dimension of consistency which Van Kaam says Jesus, as a mature personality, possessed: Jesus was sensitive to the immediate needs of people around him. The stability and consistency with the ultimate life situation which characterizes a mature personality does not mean that such a one is unmoved, unaffected, untouched by the reality of the moment." Indeed, he may be deeply moved by events, while at the same time he maintains even-mindedness." This sounds contradictory but, according to Van Kaam, "a real person is a living paradox, a synthesis of traits which seem to exclude one another. In this case, the serenity in the depths of his being does not exclude profound sensitivity and spontaneity on other levels of existence." This paradox is most striking in the life of Jesus. Van Kaam continues:

> How profoundly [Jesus] was moved by the suffering of men. He wept over Jerusalem and over the death of Lazarus. He could be

moved by holy anger, as when he ejected the venders from the Temple. His encounters with His friends and disciples were pervaded by an exquisite tenderness. In the Garden of Olives He was terrified by the thought of the suffering that was awaiting Him. And still this sensitive, deeply emotional Man maintained in the core of His being an infinite poise, an unshakable serenity, an orientation of perception and purpose that never gave way under the torrents of His feelings. The direction of His will kept the same course in spite of the movements of His heart. His feelings did not change His basic orientation, but humanized the way in which He implemented this orientation in daily life.[6]

The combining of these two indomintable traits — the unshakable orientation to his destiny, and the sensitivity of heart to the immediate needs of people — is one of the sublime achievements of Jesus. While the records clearly display the former, they also poignantly reveal the latter.

Jesus loved people. Like the rest of us, he loved those who loved him, and he enjoyed special times with them. Jesus often accepted the hospitality of his friend Lazarus and two sisters, Mary and Martha (John 11:11). "Jesus loved Martha and her sister and Lazarus" (11:5). Their home was his home away from home. His love for the Lazarus' family was noted by those who came to the funeral of Lazarus. Jesus came to Bethany after Lazarus had been dead four days. John picks up on the conversation between Mary and Jesus:

> "Lord," said Mary, "If you had been here, my brother would not have died." When Jesus saw her weeping, and the Jews who had come along with her also weeping, he was deeply moved and troubled.
>
> "Where have you laid him?" he asked.
>
> "Come and see, Lord," they replied. Jesus wept.
>
> Then the Jews said, "See how he loved him" (John 11:32-37).

Jesus loved the twelve also. On the night he was arrested he demonstrated his love in this way: "It was just before the Passover," John observes. "Jesus knew that the time had come for him to leave this world and go to the Father. Having loved his own who were in the world, he now showed them the full extent of his love." John continues:

> The evening meal was being served, and the devil had already prompted Judas Iscariot, son of Simon, to betray Jesus. Jesus knew

that the Father had put all things under his power, and that he had come from God and was returning to God, so he got up from the meal, took off his outer clothing, and wrapped a towel around his waist. After that he poured water into a basin and began to wash his disciples' feet, drying them with the towel that was wrapped around him. (13:2-5).

But Jesus loved also those he did not know. Mark records that on one occasion there were so many people "coming and going" there was no time for Jesus and his disciples to eat. So Jesus said to his disciples: "Come with me by yourselves to a quiet place and get some rest" (Mark 6:31). As they went away in a boat many people saw them leave and, knowing where they were going, ran on foot and were waiting for Jesus. When Jesus came ashore and saw the large crowd he had compassion on them because they were like sheep without a shepherd. So he began teaching them many things (6:32-34). Toward the close of the day, Matthew adds, Jesus would not allow his disciples to dismiss the crowd without first feeding them. He was concerned that they would faint on the way (Matt. 15:32).

One of the most touching demonstrations of his love for strangers took place in the city of Nain. As they approached the city gate they encountered a funeral procession. Upon learning that the dead man was the only son of a widow, Jesus stopped the procession and said to the mother, "Don't cry." He then spoke to the corpse, "Young man, I say to you, get up." The dead man sat up, and Jesus gave him back to his mother (Luke 7:11-15).

Someone has said that one true measure of greatness is the way a person treats "little" people. In the minds of most, the littlest of people would be children. Jesus loved children and made time for them in his schedule. It seems that a person with as important a mission as Jesus' would not have had time for someone as seemingly insignificant as a child. But not so. Mark records that people were bringing little children to Jesus to have him touch them, but the disciples rebuked them. "Let the little children come to me, and do not hinder them," said Jesus, "for the kingdom of God belongs to such as these . . ." And he took the children in his arms, put his hands on them and blessed them (Mark 10:13-16).

Jesus seems to have been fascinated by children — by their games (Luke 7:32); by their simplicity (Luke 18:17); fascinated perhaps just because they were children, and little and delightful. Perhaps he had not forgotten that he himself was once a child, and that there was more than a little of the child in him still. Matthew (21:15) says children took part in the triumphal entry of Jesus into Jerusalem. And, clear as he was on how little the Hosannas of the grown people meant, Jesus seems to have enjoyed the children's part in the strange scene.[7]

Jesus showed uncommon kindness to another person of seemingly minor importance: the thief who died beside him. When the thief asked Jesus to remember him when he came in his kingdom, Jesus replied, "Today, you will be with me in Paradise" (Luke 23:43). Thus, for a nameless, useless and guilty human, Jesus showed special attention and kindness.

And then for the soldiers who executed him, Jesus prayed: "Father, forgive them, for they do not know what they are doing" (Luke 23:34). Thus the executed became an advocate for his executors. He had taught others that they should pray for their persecutors. But now it was he who was being tested. The consistency between his teachings and his life is nowhere more obvious than on this occasion. Out of all of Jesus' associations there shines a consistent courtesy and an unfailing respect for the individual.

It was not that he was above the temptation to be otherwise. The very first of his signs reveals a struggle between his commitment to his ultimate mission and his commitment to the immediate needs of people. It took place in Cana in Galilee at a wedding feast (John 4:1-11). Jesus, his mother, and his disciples attended the banquet. In the course of the festivities Mary, with some expectations attached, informed Jesus that the host had run out of wine. Jesus got the message but had not planned on demonstrating his power so early. He replied, "O woman, what has this to do with you and me? My hour has not yet come." It seems he was tempted to dismiss the immediate human need which interfered with the timing of his ultimate purpose. So he had to make a decision; and he decided to adjust the timing of his larger ministry to accommodate the immediate needs of people. Thus he committed himself to the dual orientation which characterized his entire ministry.

In this respect, there exists in the gospel records a pattern which speaks eloquently of Jesus' consistency in relationships. There is an ever-recurring framework over which the canvas of Jesus' life was stretched. It is an almost, if not totally, universal plot that is employed repeatedly throughout the literature and drama of all peoples of every age, but nowhere more poignantly than in the life of Jesus. It would be difficult to imagine any plot holding our interest which did not introduce the three principal characters: 1) the victim, 2) the villian and 3) the hero. Here is the familiar, age-old story:

Scene One: The victim, a widow, is struggling to provide for her two small children by working the farm her deceased husband left her. She works on tirelessly, unaware of the dark clouds gathering.

Scene Two: The plot thickens. The villian, who lives off other people and profits from their loss, rides up to the farm, knocks on the door and announces to the widow that he holds a mortgage on the farm. He demands payment at once or he will foreclose.

Scene Three: The hero comes to the rescue. The villain is exposed, and the widow in distress is rescued.

How many books of fiction, stage plays, operas and movies have been developed around this theme? They are too numerous to count. The theme is basic to the ancient Odyssey and Antigone. It appears in Shakespear's classical dramas of *Othello, Hamlet* and *Macbeth* and the old silent movies in which the villain, twirling his moustache, ties the damsel to the railroad track only to be "foiled again" by the hero of the story. It is the plot of Christopher Marlowe's *Dr. Faustus* and the villainy of Moriarity in the Sherlock Holmes' mysteries. It appears in Puccini's *Tosca* and Bethoven's *Fidelo*. From *Paradise Lost* to Popeye's rescuing Olive Oil from Brutus' lecherous grasp, this familiar theme is the stock and trade of literature and theater, whether ancient or modern, classical or "B" grade cinema.

The same age-old plot appears throughout the gospel story. Jesus' consistent relationships are worked out in this familiar framework. Broadly speaking, the world is the victim, Satan is the villain, and Jesus is the hero. The theme recurs again and again. Space won't allow a complete listing, but a few examples will give an idea of the frequency of this plot in the gospels.

John 2:13-22 — Jesus steps in between the villain temple authorities and the victimized worshippers being robbed by them.

John 4:1-42 — Jesus acts to eliminate sexual and ethnic prejudice by ignoring the local taboos existing at the time and helping a sinful woman regain self-respect.

John 4:46-54 — Jesus, the hero, provides relief to a grief-stricken father by overcoming the villain, Death.

John 5:1-18 — Jesus comes to the rescue of the cripple at Bethzatha pool in the face of official resistance.

John 8:1-11 — Jesus heroically takes the side of the oppressed adulteress against her accusers, the Pharisees.

John 9:1-39 — Jesus heals the blind man and stands between him and the oppressive religious leaders.

John 11:1-57 — At risk to his own safety, Jesus returns to Judea to rescue his friend Lazarus from the villain, Death.

Generally, all Jesus' healings display this plot and it's three main characters: victim, villain and hero.

But there are other incidents in Jesus' life, not involving physical healing, in which the plot is evident:

John 12:1-8 — Jesus takes the side of Mary and rescues her from the criticism of his own disciples.

Luke 7:36-50 — Jesus dramatically takes the side of the uninvited woman in Simon the Pharisee's house. The woman is the victim, Simon is the villain, and Jesus is the hero. What a dramatic scene!

Luke 10:38-42 — Jesus gently defends Mary from the incensed accusations of her own sister Martha.

Luke 23:39-44 — Jesus grants reprieve to the guilty thief.

Luke 23:34 — Jesus intercedes for his executors.

The plot can be detected also in some of Jesus' parables. One example is the parable of the Prodigal Son in Luke 15:11-32. The father stands between the prodigal (victim of his own sins) and his present adversary (his older brother). The occasion for this parable was yet another example of Jesus standing between the victimized sinners of his day and the religious villains who were oppressing them. It was because the Pharisees and the scribes murmured, saying, "This man receives sinners and eats with them" (Luke 15:1, 2) that Jesus told the parable of the prodigal son and his heroic father.

Another example is the parable of the Good Samaritan (Luke 10:29-37). The parable depicts the victim being rescued from the robbers by the Samaritan hero.

Thus the plot which dominates the world's literature provided the framework for the life of Jesus. Jesus found himself cast consistently in the role of the hero standing between the oppressed and the oppressor.

How did Jesus come to such an unwavering dedication to someone else's plan for his life? How did he become so obsessed by it that on one occasion he confessed, "My meat is to do the will of him who sent me, and to accomplish his work" (John 4:34). This commitment seems to have been rooted in a total awareness of his unique relationship with God. Jesus seems to have lived in a total consciousness of God's love for him: "The reason the Father loves me is that I lay down my life — only to take it up again" (10:17). "As the Father has loved me, so I have loved you. . . . If you obey my commands, you will remain in my love, just as I have obeyed my Father's commands and remain in his love" (15:9, 10). He felt so totally clothed in the love of God that he described his relationship with God as being "one with him." In his intercessory prayer Jesus prayed,

> My prayer is not for [the twelve] alone. I pray also for those who will believe in me through their message, that all of them may be one, Father, just as you are in me and I am in you. . . . May they be brought to complete unity to let the world know that you sent me and have loved them as you have loved me. . . . (John 17:20-23).

In the same prayer he claimed God's love for him existed before the origin of the world: "Father, I want those you have given me to be with me where I am, and to see my glory, the glory you have given me because you loved me before the creation of the world" (17:24).

We saw in the previous chapter the essential part that love plays in the development of the healthy and mature human psyche. It should not be surprising, therefore, that this one whose life showed complete consistency with the purpose of life should also show total awareness of being loved by the Source of life. Neither should it be surprising that one who was so confident of being loved by the Source of life should teach as his basic philosophy: "Love the Lord your God with all your heart, and with all your soul, and with all your mind;" and "Love your neighbor as yourself."

The cross of Jesus was the common denominator and perfect illustration of the complete consistency of Jesus' life. His love for God and God's plan and his love for man and man's immediate need find perfect fulfillment in the cross. They were one and the same thing. Malcom Muggeridge observed, "The point of the cross *is* the point of life." Jesus' ultimate purpose was to lay down his life; his immediate application to the daily human situation was the same. He lived the way he died, and he died the way he lived. He laid down his life long before he came to Golgotha. He simply demonstrated in his death what he had already fully documented in his life.

This section, entitled, "The Undeniables," began with an assessment of Jesus which, perhaps, you personally could not endorse at the time:

> No single influence has more greatly affected the moral and ethical standards of the world than Jesus of Nazareth. . . . One thing is certain: Jesus of Nazareth is at least singularly unique, timely, timeless and, acclaimed by both friend and foe alike, an elevating influence of the highest order.

Having explored this section rather extensively, perhaps you now can see how that assessment could reasonably have been made and can now concur with it. The "Undeniables" were described originally as the "less threatening caverns of evidence" and were recommended as our first area of exploration.

Now, under the heading of "The Unbelievables," we approach the "more difficult passages and the deep waters." This stretch of our exploration will require, as part of our equipment, a stout heart and an open mind in order to see it through to the end.

Let's be on our way.

1. Hans Heinrich Wendt, *The Teachings of Jesus* (New York: Charles Scribner's Sons, 1899), I, p. 114.

2. H. H. Henson, *Christian Morality* (Oxford: Clarendon Press, 1936), p. 301.

3. Adrian Van Kaam, *Religion and Personality* (Garden City, N.Y.: Image Books/Doubleday & Company, Inc., 1968), p. 70.

4. Ibid., p. 70, 71.

5. Hugh J. Schonfield, *The Passover Plot* (New York: Bernard Geis Associates, 1965), p. 137.

6. Ibid.

7. Glover, Op. cit., p. 94.

SECTION III
THE
UNBELIEVABLES

9

Jesus'
Signs

Hopefully, after reading the preceding section, you have come to agree with the Scandanavian sceptic who admitted openly, "I found Jesus to be 100 percent correct."

Let's pick up the young man's story where we left off. It may be that, as we lift our torch at the entrance to the next section and make our way through the opening entitled, "The Unbelievables," his story will help you identify where you are in your own search.

In reply to the young man's "100 percent correct" endorsement of Jesus' teachings, I asked him,

"Why, then, are you not a disciple of Jesus?"

He thought for a moment and replied, "I don't know."

I didn't know either, but I knew he was allowing me to walk on holy ground. He was permitting me to see into his heart.

Then I asked him, "What do you think of Jesus' miracles?"

He shot right back, "O, I don't spend any time thinking about the miracles!" He said later, "I could really believe in Jesus if it were not for the miracles."

* * * * * *

Obviously, the young man was treating the miracles as a problem unworthy of consideration. But as Bernard Ramm observes,

Miracles will always fare poorly in deliberations if treated only as problems in science and history. The axioms of science and history are not readily assimilated to miracles because of the very nature of a miracle. That is, both science and history work on the axiom of continuity, and the miracle is essentially a discontinuity. Therefore, additional axioms are necessary . . . that re-inforce, fortify and interpret the factual claims to miracles.

Whether the recorded miracles are in fact incredible (not to be believed) or just astonishingly out of the ordinary must be determined by other factors or "additional axioms." However, for our present purpose it is sufficient simply to relate the events as recorded and reserve the additional axioms for a later chapter.

The signs of Jesus comprise the first major category in the general area designated "The Unbelievables." The use of the term "unbelievables" is not intended to indicate that the recorded events cannot be believed, or that they are unreliable. Rather, the term refers to those events attributed to Jesus which reside outside our experience. We cannot personally vouch for them — we were not there when they allegedly occurred. Obviously this imposes upon the reader some restrictions, but we have no choice but to work within the limitations of the available evidence.

What does this mean? First, it means that, for those of us of the 20th century, the out-of-the-ordinary deeds attributed to Jesus can be neither proved nor disproved by scientific method. They lie outside the realm of empirical proof. Second, it means that, in their initial impact, the deeds under consideration tend (as does all testimony of extra-experiential events) to make the reader skeptical. I see no way of avoiding this. It is only normal for us to be skeptical about reported events which lie outside the realm of our experience.

Consequently, in the course of this investigation, we will consider the signs and claims of Jesus essentially as "anti-evidence." They are presented as material with negative impact — as evidence that is a liability, not an asset, to the credibility of Jesus. At face value the signs and claims of Jesus cause the reader to say in his heart, "That's incredible! I don't believe that." It is in this regard that J. Gresham Machen observes: "In one sense . . . miracles are a hindrance to faith —

but whoever thought to the contrary? It may certainly be admitted that if the New Testament had no miracles in it, it would be far easier to believe . . . but the trouble is, it would not be worth believing."[1] There are some thirty-five miracles recorded as having been performed by Jesus in the presence of witnesses. Some are recorded by only one gospel writer, others by two, still others by three, and only one by all four of the writers. Some of the accounts are similar but not identical, suggesting perhaps that either the accounts are duplicates with different details or are different events with similar circumstances. One cannot always be sure; however, they all are recorded as actual events in the life of the man Jesus who, by any standard, is astonishingly out of the ordinary.

The synoptic gospels (Matthew, Mark and Luke) record the signs of Jesus in a decidedly different manner from the Gospel of John. They provide more nearly a running account than a detailed commentary. Mark, in particular, passes quickly from one deed to another without taking time for reflection or implication. John, however, looks at the implications as well as the deeds. Consequently, the Synoptics record less about more events while John records more about fewer events. We will look at this astonishingly out-of-the-ordinary man by viewing first some abbreviated reports by Matthew, Mark and Luke, then later pause with John to see more of the details and implications. The unabridged accounts of these events are referenced at the end of each event.

IN THE SYNOPTICS

First, let's notice the signs reported in common by the three parallel writers. There are ten; most are healings. Jesus heals:

PETER'S MOTHER-IN-LAW — **He touched her hand and the fever left her, and she got up and began to wait on him** (Matt. 8:14ff; Mk. 1:30ff; Lk. 4:38ff).

TWO DEMON-POSSESSED MEN — When he arrived at the other side of in the region of the Gadarenes, two demon-possessed men coming from the tombs met him. . . . The demons begged Jesus, "If you drive us out, send us into the herd of pigs."

Jesus said to them, "**Go!**" **So they came out and went into the pigs, and the whole herd rushed down the steep bank into the lake and died in the water.** (Matt. 8:28ff; Mk. 5:1ff; Lk. 8:28).

A LEPER — A man with leprosy came and knelt before him and said, "Lord, if you are willing, you can make me clean."

Jesus reached out his hand and touched the man. "I am willing," he said. "Be Clean!" Immediately he was cured of his leprosy. (Matt. 8:2ff; Mk. 1:40ff; Lk. 5:12ff).

JAIRUS' DAUGHTER — A ruler of the synagogue came and knelt before him and said, "My daughter is at the point of death. But come and put your hand on her, and she will live" . . . **After the crowd had been put outside, he went in and took the girl by the hand, and she got up.** (Matt. 9:18ff; Mk. 5:23ff; Lk. 8:41ff).

A HEMORRHAGING WOMAN — **And a woman was there who had been subject to bleeding for twelve years, but no one could heal her. She came up behind him and touched the edge of his cloak, and immediately her bleeding stopped.**

Then he said to her, "**Daughter, your faith has healed you. Go in peace**" (Luke 8:43ff; Matt. 9:20ff; Mk. 5:25ff).

A PARALYZED MAN — When Jesus saw their faith, he said to the paralytic, "Son, your sins are forgiven . . . **I tell you, get up, take up your mat and go home." He got up, took his mat and walked out in full view of them all.** (Mk. 2:1ff; Matt. 9:1ff; Lk. 5:18ff).

A WITHERED HAND — Going on from that place, he went into their synagogue, and a man with a shriveled hand was there. **Then he said to the man, "Stretch out your hand." So he stretched it out and it was completely restored, just as sound as the other.** (Matt. 12:9ff; Mk. 3:1ff; Lk. 6:6ff).

AN EPILEPTIC CHILD — A man in the crowd called out, "Teacher, I beg you to look at my son . . . Even while the boy was coming, the demon threw him to the ground in a convulsion. **But Jesus rebuked the evil spirit, healed the boy and gave him back to his father.** (Luke 9:38ff; Matt. 17:14ff; Mk. 9:14ff).

A BLIND MAN — So they called to the blind man, "Cheer up! On your feet! He's calling you." Throwing his cloak aside, he jumped to his feet and came to Jesus.

"What do you want me to do for you?" Jesus asked him.

The blind man said, "Rabbi, I want to see."

"Go," said Jesus, "your faith has healed you." Immediately he received his sight and followed Jesus along the road (Mk. 10:46ff; Matt. 20:29ff; Lk. 18:35).

JESUS CALMS THE STORM — Then he got up and rebuked the winds and the waves, and it was completely calm. (Matt. 8:23ff; Mk. 4:37ff; Lk. 8:33ff).

IN MATTHEW AND MARK

Three signs are recorded jointly by Matthew and Mark:

JESUS HEALS DAUGHTER OF CANAANITE WOMAN — A Canaanite woman from that vicinity came to him, crying out, "Lord, Son of David, have mercy on me! My daughter is suffering terribly from demon possession" . . .

Then Jesus answsered, "Woman, you have great faith. Your request is granted." And her daughter was healed from that very hour (Matt. 15:22ff; Mk. 7:24).

JESUS FEEDS FOUR THOUSAND — He told the crowd to sit down on the ground. When he had taken the seven loaves and given thanks, he broke them and gave them to his disciples to set before the people, and they did so. They had a few small fish as well; he gave thanks for them also and told the disciples to distribute them. The people ate and were satisfied. Afterwards the disciples picked up seven baskets full of broken pieces that were left over. About four thousand men were present (Mk. 8:1; Matt. 15:32ff).

JESUS CURSES THE FIG TREE — Seeing in the distance a fig tree in leaf, he went to find out if it had any fruit. When he reached it, however, he found nothing but leaves because it was not the season for figs. Then he said to the tree, "May no one ever eat fruit from you again." And his disciples heard him say it. . . . In the morning, as they went along, they saw the fig tree withered from the roots. (Mk. 11:12-14, 20;21; Matt. 21:19ff).

IN MATTHEW AND LUKE

Two signs are recorded jointly by Matthew and Luke:

JESUS HEALS CENTURION'S SERVANT — He entered Capernaum. There a centurion's servant, whom his master valued highly, was sick and about to die. The centurion heard of Jesus and sent some of the elders of the Jews to him, asking him to come and heal his servant. . . . **Then the men who had been sent returned to the house and found the servant well** (Luke 7:1ff; Matt. 8:5).

A BLIND, MUTE DEMONIAC — **Then they brought him a demon-possessed man who was blind and mute, and Jesus healed him, so that he could both talk and see.** (Matt. 12:22-23; Lk. 11:14).

IN MARK AND LUKE

Only one sign is recorded jointly by Mark and Luke:

JESUS HEALS A DEMONIAC — In the synagogue there was a man possessed by a demon, an evil spirit. He cried out at the top of his voice, "Ha! What do you want with us, Jesus of Nazareth? Have you come to destroy us? I know who you are — the Holy One of God."

"**Be quiet!**" Jesus said sternly. "**Come out of him!**" **Then the demon threw the man down before them all and came out without injuring him** (Lk. 4:33ff; Mk. 1:23ff).

IN MATTHEW

One sign is recorded exclusively by Matthew:

JESUS CURES TWO BLIND MEN — **Then he touched their eyes and said, "According to your faith it will be done to you;" and their sight was restored** (Matt. 9:27ff).

IN MARK

Two are recorded solely by Mark:

JESUS HEALS A DEAF MUTE — **After he took him aside away from the crowd, Jesus put his fingers into the man's ears. Then he spit and touched the man's tongue. He looked up to heaven and with a deep sigh said to him, "Ephphatha!" (which means, "Be opened!"). At this, the man's ears were opened, his tongue was loosened and he began to speak plainly** (Mk. 7:31ff).

A BETHSAIDAN BLIND MAN — They came to Bethsaida, and some people brought a blind man and begged Jesus to touch him. . . . **Jesus put his hands on the man's eyes. Then his eyes were opened, his sight was restored, and he saw everything clearly.** (Mk. 8:22-26).

IN LUKE

Luke, a physician, records more cases of healings than any other writer. Five of these are recorded solely by him. They are:

JESUS RAISES WIDOW'S SON — As he approached the town gate, a dead person was being carried out — the only son of his mother, and she was a widow. **Then he went up and touched the coffin, and those carrying it stood still. He said, "Young man, I say to you, get up!" The dead man sat up and began to talk, and Jesus gave him back to his mother.** (Lk. 7:11-16).

JESUS HEALS WOMAN OF SCOLIOSIS — **When Jesus saw her, he called her forward and said to her, "Woman, you are set free from your infirmity." Then he put his hands on her, and immediately she straightened up and praised God** (Lk. 13:10).

A MAN WITH DROPSY — **There in front of him was a man suffering from dropsy. . . . So taking hold of the man, he healed him and sent him away** (Lk. 14:1-4).

TEN LEPERS — **When he saw them, he said, "Go, show yourselves to the priests." And as they went, they were cleansed** (Lk. 17:11).

MALCHUS — When Jesus' followers saw what was going to happen, they said, "Lord, should we strike with our swords?" **And one of them struck the servant of the high priest, cutting off his right ear. But Jesus answered, "No more of this!" And he touched the man's ear and healed him** (Lk. 22:47).

Luke also records:

JESUS AND THE CATCH OF FISH — When he had finished speaking, he said to Simon, **"Put out into deep water, and let down the nets for a catch."**
When they had done so, they caught such a large number of fish that their nets began to break. So they signaled their partners in the other boat to come and help them, and they came and filled both boats so full that they began to sink (Lk. 5:4ff).

Having looked at the record of Jesus' signs recorded by Matthew, Mark and Luke, we turn now to consider John's interesting and unique listing of Jesus' works.

John recorded very few (eight of the thirty-five) of those out-of-the-ordinary deeds of Jesus. Although John recorded fewer signs, it is significant that his gospel is built around those signs: "Jesus did many other miraculous signs in the presence of his disciples, which are not recorded in this book. But these are written that you may believe . . ." (John 20:30-31). And though he records fewer signs, the ones he does record are told in great detail, involving (as in John 9) an entire chapter.

John's use of the word "sign" to refer to the extra-ordinary deeds of Jesus, implies that the deeds were to be viewed as a means to the greater end of revealing the identity of the one who performed them. For some people the signs were not sufficient evidence to produce faith, for "Even after Jesus had done all these miraculous signs in their presence, they still would not believe in him" (John 12:37). Many others, "even among the leaders believed in him. But because of the Pharisees they would not confess their faith for fear they would be put out of the synagogue . . ." (12:42). However, "many people saw the miraculous signs he was doing and believed in his name" (2:23).

It was to that same end that John recorded the deeds of Jesus for his reading audience: "that [they] may believe that Jesus is the Christ, the son of God . . ." (20:30-31). With that purpose clearly in mind, John sets out to share with the reader what he claims to have observed while in the company of Jesus.

JESUS CHANGES WATER TO WINE. On the third day a wedding took place at Cana in Galilee. Jesus' mother was there, and Jesus and his disciples had also been invited to the wedding. When the wine was gone, Jesus' mother said to him, "They have no more wine" . . .

Jesus said to the servants, **"Fill the jars with water;"** so they filled them to the brim.

Then he told them, **"Now draw some out and take it to the master of the banquet."**

They did so, and the master of the banquet tasted the water that had been turned into wine. He did not realize where it had come from, though the servants who had drawn the water knew. **Then he called the bridegroom aside and said, "Everyone brings out the choice wine first and then the cheap-**

er wine after the guests have had too much to drink; but you have saved the best till now" (Jn. 2:1-11).

JESUS HEALS THE OFFICIAL'S SON. Once more he visited Cana in Galilee, where he had turned water into wine. And there was a certain royal official whose son lay sick at Capernaum. When this man heard that Jesus had arrived in Galilee from Judea, he went to him and begged him to come and heal his son, who was close to death . . .

The royal official said, "Sir, come down before my child dies."

Jesus replied, "**You may go. Your son will live.**" The man took Jesus at his word. While he was still on the way, his servants met him with the news that his boy was living. When he inquired as to the time when his son had gotten better, they said to him, "The fever left him yesterday at the seventh hour."

Then the father realized that this was the exact time at which Jesus had said to him, "Your son will live" (Jn. 4:46-53).

JESUS HEALS A CRIPPLE. Some time later, Jesus went up to Jerusalem for a feast of the Jews. Now there is in Jerusalem near the Sheep Gate a pool, which in Aramaic is called Bethesda and which is surrounded by five covered colonnades. Here a great number of disabled people used to lie — the blind, the lame, the paralyzed. One who was there had been an invalid for thirty-eight years. When Jesus saw him lying there and learned that he had been in this condition for a long time, he . . . said to him, "**Get up! Pick up your mat and walk.**" At once the man was cured; he picked up his mat and walked (Jn. 5:1-9).

JESUS FEEDS THE FIVE THOUSAND. When Jesus looked up and saw a great crowd coming toward him, he said to Philip, "Where shall we buy bread for these people to eat?" . . . Another of his disciples, Andrew, Simon Peter's brother, spoke up, "Here is a boy with five small barley loaves and two small fish, but how far will they go among so many?"

Jesus said, "Have the people sit down" . . . **Jesus then took the loaves, and gave thanks, and distributed to those who were seated as much as they wanted. He did the same with the fish.**

When they had all had enough to eat, he said to his disciples, "Gather the pieces that are left over. Let nothing be wasted." So they gathered them and filled twelve baskets with the pieces of the five barley loaves left over by those who had eaten (Jn. 6:1ff; See also Matt. 14:15ff; Mk. 6:30ff; Lk. 9:10ff).

JESUS WALKS ON THE SEA. When evening came, his disciples went down to the lake, where they got into a boat and set off across the lake for Capernaum. By now it was dark, and Jesus had not yet joined them. A strong wind was blowing, and the waters grew rough. **When they had rowed three or four miles, they saw Jesus approaching the boat, walking on the water; and they were terrified. But he said to them, "It is I; don't be afraid."** Then they were willing to take him into the boat . . . (Jn. 6:16ff; See also Matt. 14:25ff and Mk. 6:48).

JESUS HEALS A MAN BORN BLIND. As he went along, he saw a man blind from birth . . . **[Jesus] spit on the ground, made some mud with the saliva, and put it on the man's eyes. "Go," he told him, "wash in the pool of Siloam." . . . So the man went and washed, and came home seeing** (Jn. 9:1-6).

JESUS RAISES LAZARUS FROM THE DEAD. **"Jesus called in a loud voice, "Lazarus, Come out!" The dead man came out, his hands and feet wrapped with strips of linen, and a cloth around his face.**

Jesus said to them, "Take off the grave clothes and let him go." (Jn. 11:38-46).

Recorded by all four evangelists and occupying a place all its own as the central event upon which the entirety of the Christian claim rests, is the alleged resurrection of Jesus from the dead. It is recorded by all four writers. The most abbreviated account of the event (Mark 16:1-8) is used here without comment.

JESUS IS RAISED FROM THE DEAD. When the Sabbath was over, Mary Magdalene, Mary the mother of Jesus, and Salome bought spices so that they might anoint Jesus' body. Very early on the first day of the week, just after sunrise, they were on their way to the tomb and they asked each other, "Who will roll the stone away from the entrance of the tomb?"

But when they looked up, they saw that the stone, which was very large, had been rolled away. As they entered the tomb, they saw a young man dressed in a white robe sitting on the right side, and they were alarmed.

"Don't be alarmed," he said. "You are looking for Jesus the Nazarene, who was crucified. He has risen! (Mark 16:1-8).

One final event brings this chapter to a close. Mark and Luke record:

JESUS' ASCENSION — When he had led them out to the vicinity of Bethany, he lifted up his hands and blessed them. **While he was blessing them, he left them and was taken up into heaven.** (Lk. 24:50-52).

This brings to a conclusion the out-of-the-ordinary deeds attributed to Jesus in the Gospels. Recorded with an objectivity that borders on detachment and an unembroidered simplicity that informs, not excites, the material commends itself for further study.

We turn our attention now to that part of the evidence which is probably the most startling of all: Jesus' outright claims of deity; that he was of another realm altogether (John 8:23), and that divine. Though most everyone would prefer not to struggle with such claims, by this point in our search, wouldn't you agree that Jesus deserves to be heard? Perhaps Jesus' claims will shed unexpected and indispensable light on the dilemma presented by his totally unique life.

---

1. J. Gresham Machen, *Christianity and Liberalism* (Grand Rapids: Wm. B. Eerdmans Publishing Co., 1946), pp. 102, 103.

10

Jesus' Claims

If the signs of Jesus pose a problem for the searcher, the claims of Jesus may pose an even greater one. And not just for those living today. Jesus' claims were the major hurdle for his contemporaries as well. It was his claims, not his signs, that provoked the angry resistance reported in detail in the gospel records. Jesus said to them, "I have shown you many great miracles from the Father. For which of these do you stone me?" "We are not stoning you for any of these," replied the Jews, "but for blasphemy, because you, a mere man, claim to be God" (John 10:32-33).

Though his signs provoked criticism, heated debate and strenuous opposition from his enemies, it was not the signs which were brought as evidence against him at his trial. They were never mentioned; rather, it was his claims. The climax of Jesus' trial before the Jewish Supreme Court was reached when, in response to the demand of the High Priest, Jesus claimed to be the Messiah, the Son of God. For this he was sentenced to death.

His claims prove a hurdle for his hearers, then and now. Whereas being an eye witness to his deeds gave the viewers an advantage, being an ear witness to his claims gave the hearers no such advantage. In and of themselves, Jesus' assertions about himself were just as intangible and nebulous to his contemporaries[1] as they are to the modern reader. To those who witnessed them his deeds were at least tangible evidence. Not so his claims. They have never been tangible. By their very nature claims require evidence beyond themselves to establish their credibility.

And such evidence Jesus seemed always willing to give. He recognized that claims have no validity in the absence of proof. Unbelievables require undeniables if credibility is to be established. We noted above (see Chapter 3) that this approach to evidence was precisely the approach Jesus used. We cited specifically the event of the healing of the paralytic. On that occasion (Mark 2:1-12) Jesus effectively placed his adversaries in between what could not be proved (his authority to forgive sins) and what could not be denied (his power to heal the paralytic).

John records a similar occasion on which Jesus claimed:

> "I and the Father are one." Again the Jews picked up stones to stone him, but Jesus said to them, "I have shown you many great miracles from the Father. For which of these do you stone me?"
>
> "We are not stoning you for any of these," replied the Jews, "but for blasphemy, because you, a mere man, claim to be God."
>
> Jesus answered them, "Is it not written in your Law, 'I have said you are gods'? If he called them 'gods,' to whom the word of God came — and the Scripture cannot be broken — what about the one whom the Father set apart as his very own and sent into the world? Why then do you accuse me of blasphemy because I said, 'I am God's Son'? Do not believe me unless I do what my Father does. But if I do it, even though you do not believe me, believe the evidence of the miracles, that you may learn and understand that the Father is in me, and I in the Father" (John 10:30-38; see also 5:31-36).

Even with the Twelve, Jesus employed this line of reasoning. On the night of his arrest he challenged them:

> Don't you believe that I am in the Father, and that the Father is in me? The words I say to you are not just my own. Rather, it is the Father, living in me, who is doing his work. Believe me when I say that I am in the Father and the Father is in me; or at least believe on the evidence of the miracles themselves (John 14:10, 11).

Had Jesus been no more than a miracle worker, it is doubtful his countrymen would have executed him. They might have disliked him, but there would have been no cause to kill him.

Not until his accusers were required to view his deeds in the light of his claims did the implications force them to execute him. Jesus was not a mere wonder-worker; according to every piece of available evidence he was a man who also made startling claims about himself and appealed constantly and without hesitation to his works as proof of the truthfulness of those claims. He knew that claims could not bear their own weight. But when that which could not easily be believed was spoken in the context of what could not be reasonably denied, the issue was settled.

"Settled?" you may be thinking. "Then the verdict must be negative, for the majority of his own people did not believe him." This is true. Sixty years after Jesus' execution John reflected upon that rejection: "He came to his own people and those who were his own did not receive him . . ." (John 1:11). "Though he had done so many signs before them, yet they did not believe him . . ." (12:37).

"You mean to tell me," you may be saying, "that the majority of Jesus' contemporaries who weighed his claims in the light of his deeds did, in fact, reject him?" That's right. At least the leaders did initially. Even a surface reading of the records reveals this. This may leave you a bit confused and cause you to ask, "If the leaders of his own nation who saw him and heard him rejected him, why should I — indeed, how *can* I — believe him?"

You can believe Jesus the same way one comes to believe Heinrich Schliemann and his associate Dorpfeld excavated ancient Troy: by examining the evidence with an open mind. And on this point, a contemporary of Schliemann made an observation regarding the opposition Schliemann aroused. I quote it here as having value for us as we consider the claims of Jesus and the inevitable opposition they provoke.

> It is of little wonder if at first the discoverer who had so rudely shocked the settled prejudices of the historians should have met with the storm of indignant opposition or covert attack . . . *[but] today no trained archaeologist in Greece or Western Europe doubts the main facts which Dr. Schliemann's excavations have established;* we can never again return to the ideas of ten years ago."[2] (emphasis, JSW).

So, in regard to Jesus of Nazareth: it is no wonder that he is met with a storm of indignant opposition or covert attack: he shocks the settled prejudices of all who meet him. Yet, it seems unthinkable, having observed his life and teachings and how they have elevated and shaped our very perspective on life, that we should ever be willing to return to the concepts which controlled the direction and destiny of the human race prior to his life. We would not return if we could! And I think you agree.

But we are getting ahead of ourselves. We will attempt to resolve this dilemma in Chapter 11. But for right now, having considered the general nature of claims — especially those of Jesus — we turn our attention to the claims themselves. As with the signs, we will begin by considering the claims of Jesus as recorded in Matthew, Mark and Luke — and for the same reason: the claims recorded by these three writers are not as stark, bold nor lengthy as those recorded by John. In the former the claims play a minor part, while in John's Gospel they play a major role — to the point of becoming the center of attention, the topic of conversation. In the Synoptics the claims of Jesus provoke an occasional skirmish; in John they provide the battlefield, the occasion for the conflict and the ammunition all rolled into one.

However, in the interest of preserving the flow of the record found in all four accounts, Jesus' claims recorded by John will be interspersed among his claims found in the Synoptics. As the boldness of Jesus' claims increases, the intensity of the battle between him and his opponents increases.[3] The escalation of the one coincides with the increase of the other until they terminate in the final trial of Jesus before the Sanhedran in which he claimed the ultimate and was sentenced to the ultimate.

For the sake of chronology as well as objectivity we start with those claims which, though interesting, hardly deserved having the man committed to an insane asylum or executed. They conceivably could have been made by other of history's outstanding characters. They were vague enough to provoke little resistance and innocuous enough to cause little harm. Admittedly, Jesus did not make many such claims; but there were one or two, and these appear in the Synoptics. They are:

JESUS PROMISES REWARDS TO FOLLOWERS — "One thing you lack," he said. "Go sell everything you have and give to the poor, and you will have treasure in heaven. Then come, follow me" (Mk. 10:21).

JESUS PROMISES HUNDRED-FOLD — "I tell you the truth," Jesus replied, "no one who has left home or brothers or sisters or mother or father or children or fields for me and the gospel will fail to receive a hundred times as much in this present age (homes, brothers, sisters, mothers, children and fields — and with them, persecutions) and in the age to come, eternal life" (Mk. 10:29-30).

JESUS PROMISES REST — "Come to me, all you who are weary and burdened, and I will give you rest. Take my yoke upon you and learn from me, for I am gentle and humble in heart, and you will find rest for your souls. For my yoke is easy and my burden is light" (Matt. 11:28-30).

In one form or another and to one degree or another the preceeding claims have been made by many a spiritual leader seeking a following, or even by political leaders running for office. They amounted to little more than promises and aroused little or no resistance.

The only claims recorded by John which could be considered innocuous are those in John 4. The claims were as extreme as any Jesus made, but because they were made to an individual of little importance and in a location far from the power center of Judaism, they caused little disturbance. The occasion was Jesus' conversation with the Samaritan woman at Jacob's well in Sycar:

JESUS CLAIMS TO GIVE EVERLASTING LIFE — When a Samaritan woman came to draw water, Jesus said to her, "Will you give me a drink?" . . .

The Samaritan woman said to him, "You are a Jew and I am a Samaritan woman. How can you ask me for a drink?" (For Jews do not associate with Samaritans.)

Jesus answered her, "If you knew the gift of God and who it is that asks you for a drink, you would have asked him and he would have given you living water. . . . Everyone who drinks of this water will be thirsty again, but whoever drinks the water I give him will never thirst. Indeed, the water I give him will become in him a spring of water welling up to everlasting life" (Jn. 4:10-14).

JESUS CLAIMS TO BE THE MESSIAH — The woman said, "I know that Messiah . . . is coming. When he comes, he will explain everything to us."

Then Jesus declared, "**I who speak to you am he**" (Jn. 4:7-10, 13-14, 25-26).

The remainder of Jesus' claims definitely raise the eyebrows and rule out any possibility that Jesus might be ignored or regarded as a good, but ordinary man. The remainder of the claims to which I call your attention are explicit. Time after time Jesus clearly placed himself on record in matters that could not be ignored. He claimed to be superior to both holy people and sacred places. He claimed to transcend time — to be a part of eternity; to be the giver of life and the conqueror of death; to be savior and judge. He even claimed to be the extension of God himself. Let's notice now those explicit claims:

JESUS CLAIMS TO BE GREATER THAN:

Jonah — ". . . **and now one greater than Jonah is here**" (Matt. 12:41; See also Lk. 11:32).

Solomon — ". . . **and now one greater than Solomon is here**" (Matt. 12:42; See also Lk. 11:31).

The Temple — "**I tell you that one greater than the temple is here**" (Matt. 12:1-7).

JESUS CLAIMS AUTHORITY IN THE TEMPLE — When it was almost time for the Jewish Passover, Jesus went up to Jerusalem. In the temple court he found men selling cattle, sheep and doves, and others sitting at tables exchanging money. So he made a whip out of cords, and drove all from the temple area, both sheep and cattle; he scattered the coins of the money-changers and overturned their tables. To those who sold doves, he said, "**Get these out of here! How dare you turn my Father's house into a market!**" (Jn. 2:13-21) (See also Matt. 21:12-13 and Mk. 11:16).

JESUS CLAIMS HIS WORKS ARE THE WORKS OF GOD — "**My Father is always at his work to this very day, and I, too, am working. . . . I tell you the truth, the Son can do nothing by himself. He can do only what he sees his Father doing, because whatever the Father does the Son also does.**" (Jn. 5:17-20, 36-38).

JESUS CLAIMS TO BE LORD OF THE SABBATH — "**For the Son of Man is Lord of the Sabbath**" (Matt. 12:7-8).

JESUS CLAIMS TO BE FULFILLMENT OF PRO-
PHECY — He went to Nazareth, where he had been brought
up, and on the Sabbath day he went into the synagogue, as was
his custom. And he stood up to read . . .

Then he rolled up the scroll, gave it back to the attendant
and sat down. The eyes of everyone in the synagogue were
fastened on him, and he said to them, "**Today this scripture is
fulfilled in your hearing**" (Lk. 4:16-21).

"**These are the Scriptures that testify about me, yet you
refuse to come to me to have life**" (Jn. 5:39-40).

"**If you believed Moses, you would believe me, for he wrote
about me**" (5:45-46).

JESUS CLAIMS PRIORITY OVER FAMILY RELA-
TIONS — "**Anyone who loves his father or mother more than
me is not worthy of me; anyone who loves his son or daughter
more than me is not worthy of me.**" (Matt. 10:34-39).

JESUS CLAIMS TO BE THE JUDGE IN FINAL JUDG-
MENT — "**Many will say to me on that day, 'Lord, Lord, did
we not prophesy in your name, and in your name drive out
demons and perform many miracles?'' Then I will tell them
plainly, 'I never knew you. Away from me, you evil doers'** "
(Matt. 7:21-23).

"**The Son of Man will send out his angels, and they will
weed out of his kingdom everything that causes sin and all
who do evil. They will throw them into the fiery furnace, where
there will be weeping and grinding of teeth**" (Matt. 13:41-42).

"**For the Son of Man is going to come in his Father's glory
with his angels, and then he will reward each person according
to what he has done**" (Matt. 16:27) (See also Matt. 19:28;
25:31-34, 41).

JESUS CLAIMS HIS WORDS INDISPENSABLE TO
LIFE — "**Therefore, everyone who hears these words of mine
and puts them into practice is like a wise man who built his
house on the rock. The rain came down, the streams rose, and
the winds blew and beat against that house; yet it did not fall,
because it had its foundation on the rock. But everyone who
hears these words of mine and does not put them into practice
is like a foolish man who built his house on the sand. The rain
came down, the streams rose, and the winds blew and beat
against that house, and it fell with a great crash**" (Matt. 7:24-
27).

JESUS CLAIMS HE SPEAKS FOR GOD — "**My teach-
ing is not my own. It comes from him who sent me. If anyone**

chooses to do God's will, he will find out whether my teaching comes from God or whether I speak on my own" (Jn. 7:16-18). (See also Jn. 12:47-50).

JESUS CLAIMS TO BE THE LIGHT OF THE WORLD — When Jesus spoke again to the people, he said, "I am the light of the world. Whoever follows me will never walk in darkness, but will have the light of life" (Jn. 8:12-29).

JESUS CLAIMS TO BE FROM ABOVE — "You are from below, I am from above; you are of this world, I am not of this world" (Jn. 8:23).

JESUS CLAIMS KEY POSITION BETWEEN GOD AND HUMANS — "Whoever acknowledges me before men, I will also acknowledge him before my Father in heaven. But whoever disowns me before men, I will disown him before my Father in heaven" (Matt. 10:32-33).

The next major body of claims recorded by John are the claims involved in the so-called "Bread of Life" discourse in John 6. They are best treated as a unit in themselves, even though Jesus made other claims during the discourse. The claims contained in this discourse were possibly, to the Jewish ear, the most repulsive of all since they appeared to require cannibalism. This event has been called the "watershed" of Jesus' public ministry. It was shortly before this, at the feeding of the five thousand, that Jesus' ministry reached its peak in popular support; but upon his insistence that his followers "eat his flesh and drink his blood," many of his disciples abandoned him, and public support of Jesus plunged to its lowest point.

JESUS CLAIMS TO BE THE BREAD OF LIFE — Then Jesus declared, "I am the bread of life. He who comes to me will never go hungry, and he who believes in me will never be thirsty. . . . I am the bread of life . . . I am the living bread that came down from heaven. If a man eats of this bread, he will live forever. This bread is my flesh, which I will give for the life of the world. . . . I tell you the truth, unless you eat the flesh of the Son of Man and drink his blood, you have no life in you. Whoever eats my flesh and drinks my blood has eternal life, and I will raise him up at the last day. (Jn. 6:35-58).

The next major group of claims is contained in the latter part of John 8. If Jesus' claims in John 6 that his flesh and blood were essential to life offended the religious sensitivities of the Jews, his claims made in the so-called "Freedom" discourse in John 8 offended their national pride as well. This latter discourse contains claims that range all the way from his saying "If you will abide in my word you will be set free" to the unheard-of claim that he was the "I AM" (the special name of Jehovah, the God of Israel).

JESUS CLAIMS TO SET MEN FREE — To the Jews who had believed him, Jesus said, "**If you continue in my teaching, you are really my disciples. Then you will know the truth and the truth will set you free.**"

"**I am telling you what I have seen in the Father's presence.**"

"**Can any of you prove me guilty of sin?**"

"**I tell you the truth, if a man keeps my word, he will never see death.**"

"**Your father Abraham rejoiced at the thought of seeing my day; he saw it and was glad.**"

"**I tell you the truth,**" Jesus answered, "**before Abraham was born, I am.**" (Jn. 8:31-59).

JESUS CLAIMS TO BE THE GOOD SHEPHERD — Therefore Jesus said again, "**I tell you the truth, I am the gate for the sheep . . . whoever enters through me will be saved. He will come in and go out, and find pasture . . . I have come that they may have life, and have it to the full. I am the good shepherd . . .**" (Jn. 10:7-10).

JESUS CLAIMS TO BE ONE WITH GOD — "**I and the Father are one**" (Jn. 10:22-30).

JESUS CLAIMS TO BE THE SON OF GOD — Again the Jews picked up stones to stone him, but Jesus said to them, "I have shown you many great miracles from the Father. For which of these do you stone me?"

"We are not stoning you for any of these," replied the Jews, "but for blasphemy, because you, a mere man, claim to be God."

Jesus answered them, "Is it not written in your Law, 'I have said you are gods'? If he called them 'gods,' to whom the word of God came — and the Scripture cannot be broken — **what about the one whom the Father set apart as his very own and sent into the world? Why then do you accuse me of blasphemy because I said, 'I am God's Son'? Do not believe me unless I do what my Father does. But if I do it, even though** you do not believe me, believe the miracles, that you may learn and understand that the Father is in me, and I in the Father." Again they tried to seize him, but he escaped their grasp (Jn. 10:31-39).

JESUS ACCEPTS MESSIANIC IDENTITY — Simon Peter answered, "You are the Christ, the Son of the living God."

Jesus replied, "Blessed are you, Simon son of Jonah, for this was not revealed to you by man, but by my Father in heaven. . . . Then he warned his disciples not to tell anyone that he was the Christ (Matt. 16:13-17, 20; Mk. 8:27-30; Lk. 9:18-21).

JESUS CLAIMS POWER TO FORGIVE SINS — Now one of the Pharisees invited Jesus to have dinner with him, so he went to the Pharisee's house and reclined at the table. When a woman who lived a sinful life in that town learned that Jesus was eating at the Pharisee's house, she brought an alabaster jar of perfume, and as she stood behind him at his feet weeping, she began to wet his feet with her tears. Then she wiped them with her hair, kissed them and poured perfume on them. . . . Then Jesus said, "Your sins are forgiven." (Lk. 7:36-38, 48-49).

JESUS CLAIMS RECEIVING HIM IS EQUIVALENT TO RECEIVING GOD — "He who receives you receives me, and he who receives me receives him who sent me" (Matt. 10:40).

JESUS CLAIMS REJECTION OF HIM IS FATAL — "If anyone is ashamed of me and my words, the Son of Man will be ashamed of him when he comes in his glory and in the glory of the Father and of the holy angels" (Lk. 9:26; See also Mk. 8:38).

JESUS CLAIMS EXCLUSIVE KNOWLEDGE OF GOD — "All things have been committed to me by the Father. No one knows the Son except the Father, and no one knows the Father except the Son and those to whom the Son chooses to reveal him" (Matt. 11:27).

JESUS CLAIMS TO BE OBJECT OF PROPHECY — "But blessed are your eyes because they see, and your ears because they hear." For I tell you the truth, many prophets and righteous men longed to see what you see but did not see it, and to hear what you hear but did not hear it" (Matt. 13:16-17).

JESUS ACCEPTS MESSIANIC PRAISE — But when the chief priests and the teachers of the law saw the wonderful things he did and the children shouting in the temple area, **"Hosanna to the Son of David,"** they were indignant.

"Do you hear what these children are saying?" they asked him.

"Yes," Jesus replied, **"have you never read, 'From the lips of children and infants you have raised up praise'?"** (Matt. 21:14-16).

JESUS CLAIMS TO BE THE RESURRECTION — **"I am the resurrection and the life. He who believes in me will live, even though he dies; and whoever lives and believes in me will never die . . ."**(Jn. 11:1-2, 17-26).

JESUS CLAIMS IDENTITY WITH GOD — Then Jesus cried out, **"When a man believes in me, he does not believe in me only, but in the one who sent me. When he looks at me, he sees the one who sent me"** (Jn. 12:44-45).

The next major group of claims was made by Jesus the night before his execution. These claims were as bold as any. However, they were made in seclusion, among his own disciples and therefore did not evoke opposition because he was among friends.

JESUS CLAIMS HIS BLOOD IS FOR OTHER'S SINS — While they were eating, Jesus took bread, gave thanks and broke it, and gave it to his disciples, saying, **"Take and eat; this is my body."**

Then he took the cup, gave thanks and offered it to them, saying, "Drink from it, all of you. This is my blood of the covenant, which is poured out for many for the forgiveness of sins." (Matt. 26:26-29).

JESUS CLAIMS TO KNOW THE FATHER'S HOUSE — **"Do not let your heart be troubled. Trust in God; trust also in me. There are many rooms in my Father's house; otherwise I would have told you. I am going there to prepare a place for you. And if I go and prepare a place for you, I will come back and take you to be with me that you also may be where I am"** (Jn. 14:1-3).

JESUS CLAIMS TO BE THE ONLY WAY TO GOD — **"I am the way and the truth and the life. No one comes to the Father except through me"** (14:4-6).

JESUS CLAIMS THAT TO SEE HIM IS TO SEE GOD — "If you really knew me, you would know my Father as well. From now on, you do know him and have seen him. . . . Anyone who has seen me has seen the Father. How can you say, 'Show us the Father'? Don't you believe me that I am in the Father and the Father is in me? The words that I say to you are not just my own. Rather, it is the Father, living in me, who is doing his work. Believe me when I say that I am in the Father and the Father is in me . . ." (14:7-11a).

Virtually uninterrupted are the remaining claims Jesus made the night of his arrest. They are listed here as they appear:

"I am the true vine and my Father is the gardner" (Jn. 15:1).

"The Father will give you whatever you ask in my name" (15:16b).

"If I had not come and spoken to them, they would not be guilty of sin. Now, however, they have no excuse for their sin. He who hates me hates my Father as well" (15:22-23).

"Unless I go away, the Counselor will not come to you; but if I go away, I will send him to you" (Jn. 16:7).

"All that belongs to the Father is mine" (16:15).

"In that day you will no longer ask me anything. I tell you the truth, my Father will give you whatever you ask in my name (16:22-23).

"I have come from the Father and entered the world; now I am leaving the world and going back to the Father" (16:28).

"I have overcome the world" (16:33).

JESUS CLAIMS PRE-EXISTENCE WITH GOD — "And now, Father, glorify me in your presence with the glory I had with you before the world began" (17:5).

"Father, I want those you have given me to be with me where I am, and to see my glory, the glory you have given me because you loved me before the creation of the world" (17:24).

JESUS CLAIMS ACCESS TO LEGIONS OF ANGELS— Do you think I cannot call on my Father, and he will at once put at my disposal more than twelve legions of angels?" (Matt. 26:50-53).

Jesus made few claims in his trials before the Jewish and Roman courts. The one claim the Jewish court forced him to make brought upon him the sentence of death. The claims he made in the presence of Pilate seem to have had no damaging effect on his case. In fact, Pilate seems to have been somewhat in awe of Jesus, especially upon receiving from his wife the message, "Have nothing to do with that righteous man," and also upon learning from the Jews that Jesus "claimed to be the Son of God" (Jn. 19:7).

JESUS CLAIMS UNDER OATH TO BE THE SON OF GOD — The high Priest said to him, "I charge you under oath by the living God: Tell us if you are the Christ, the Son of God."

"Yes, it is as you say," Jesus replied. "But I say to all of you: In the future you will see the Son of Man sitting at the right hand of the Mighty One and coming on the clouds of heaven" (Matt. 26:63-64).

JESUS CLAIMS OTHER-WORLD KINGDOM — Jesus said [to Pilate], **"My kingdom is not of this world. If it were, my servants would fight to prevent my arrest by the Jews. But now my kingdom is from another place."**

"You are a king, then!" said Pilate.

Jesus answered, **"You are right in saying I am a king. In fact, for this reason I was born, and for this I came into the world . . ."** (Jn. 18:36-37).

After his resurrection Jesus made two final claims to his disciples:

JESUS CLAIMS TO BE FULFILLMENT OF PROPHE-CIES — He said to them, **"How foolish you are, and how slow of heart that you do not believe all that the prophets have spoken! Did not the Christ have to suffer these things and then enter his glory?" And beginning with Moses and all the Prophets, he explained to them what was said in the Scriptures concerning himself. . . . He said to them, "This is what I told you while I was still with you: Everything must be fulfilled that is written about me in the Law of Moses, the Prophets and the Psalms."** (Lk. 24:25-27).

JESUS CLAIMS ALL AUTHORITY IN HEAVEN AND EARTH — **"All authority in heaven and on earth has been given to me. Therefore go and make disciples of all nations,**

baptizing them in the name of the Father and of the Son and of the Holy Spirit, and teaching them to obey everything I have commanded you. And surely I will be with you always, to the very end of the age" (Matt. 28:16-20).

The preceeding list of Jesus' claims, though extensive, is not exhaustive. There are other statements which confront the reader and create the same dilemma as was created for his contemporaries who said, "He is demon-possessed and raving mad. Why listen to him?"

But others said, "These are not the sayings of a man possessed by a demon. How can a demon open the eyes of the blind?" (John 10:20-21).

And so the controversy continued, and continues, to surround Jesus' astonishing claims. The next section, entitled, "The Dilemma" should help settle the controversy.

----

1. See John 8:13.

2. A. H. Sayce, as quoted by Wood, op. cit., p. 93.

3. Lord Beaverbrook, "The Divine Propagandist," in *Great Lives Observed Jesus,* ed. Hugh Anderson (Englewood Cliffs, N.J., 1967), p. 152.

SECTION IV

THE DILEMMA
AND
CONCLUSION

11

The Dilemma

*"Faith is nothing else than reason grown courageous —
reason raised to its highest power, expanded to its widest
vision."*[1]

* * * * * *

Where has all this brought us — all this confrontive
material of Jesus' unprecedented deeds and unimaginable
claims plus all the affirmative material of his teachings and
relationships? Where has our consideration of this material
brought us? If to no other place, it has brought us to a giant
dilemma: "What shall we do with the man Jesus? What
conclusion are we to draw regarding him?"

The very fact this question is even asked may cause resent-
ment on the part of some. "Why do I need to do anything with
Jesus" — you may be asking — "any more than I need to do
anything with George Washington or Julius Caesar?" But the
last part of the question makes us aware that, indeed, we must
do something with Jesus in a special way. The very nature of
Jesus and his influence on the human scene requires us to do
something with him that is quite different from what we are
called upon to do with a Washington or a Caesar. Neither of
them makes the kind of demand upon our lives that Jesus
makes. His is more than an interesting life or an arresting

character; his life is confrontive and demanding in that the consistency of his character is coupled with the challenge of his claims. To acknowledge his character while discounting his claims is neither logical nor consistent. So the question remains: "What shall we do with Jesus?"

There are basically two options: On the one hand, if we approach the evidence from the perspective that the universe is a closed system, allowing no place for outside intervention, the dilemma is intensified and the confusion is reflected in the question: "How could someone so right in all he taught be so wrong in all he claimed about himself?" For after all, Jesus did claim to have come "from above," outside our system. And since, in a closed system, that cannot be true, his unique life and teachings pose an enormous dilemma.

On the other hand, if we (as spelunkers) approach the evidence from the standpoint that the universe may *not* be a closed system, thus allowing for intervention from outside, the dilemma is reduced significantly, and we are able to proceed in a manner consistent with the evidence. Though the adjustment in the question is slight, the shift in the implication is significant. Instead of asking, "How could someone so right in all he taught be so wrong in what he claimed?," one would ask, "Could someone so right in all he taught be wrong in what he claimed?"

There are scholars on both sides of the question. But I am convinced it is not a matter of scholarship alone. Rather, it is a matter of perspective. Though it may seem simplistic to make such an affirmation, I believe it can be shown that perspective determines the outcome of one's quest. Let me illustrate the point with this nine-dot puzzle. Examine it carefully.

●   ●   ●

●   ●   ●

●   ●   ●

Here is the challenge it presents: Take a pen and connect all nine dots with only four straight lines *without taking your pen off the paper*. Take as much time as you need to solve the puzzle, but don't look at the solution on the next page till you've given yourself a chance to solve it on your own.

How are you coming?

Chances are you are saying, "It's impossible! It can't be done!"

So it seems. Yet it can be done — very easily. But only if one is willing to go outside the natural, self-imposed limitations which one usually places on the puzzle. Turn the page now and see the solution.

The puzzle is solved when one's perception is expanded to include a broader dimension. It is necessary to break through the barrier and step outside the limitations which you, if you failed to solve it, had unconsciously imposed upon the figure.

Similarly, in order to solve the puzzle of Jesus of Nazareth, one must be willing to break through the barrier and step *outside* the limitations which our secular age has imposed on

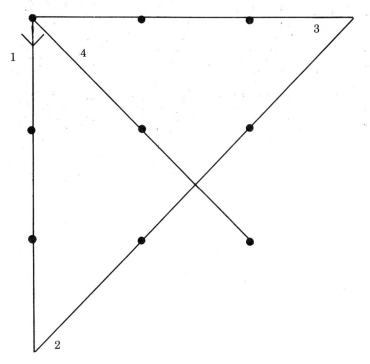

that historical figure. After all the evidence has been mined and sifted, the question still must be answered: Will I allow for the possibility of an "open" universe? Or will I insist on it being "closed"? Your answer will determine the outcome.

Assuming either position as an "a priori" fact is unscientific. A truly scientific approach never rules anything impossible. It never rules out any action. The scientific mind leaves itself open to be led wherever the evidence demands. Yet, those who investigate Jesus of Nazareth but rule out the possibility of the supernatural find themselves in an unresolvable dilemma. If the records are allowed to stand intact, we must acknowledge that Jesus openly, repeatedly and blatantly claimed to have come from God, to have come from above, to be not of this world. How does one deal fairly with a man who claimed to have come from God, whose extra-ordinary deeds are matter-of-factly recorded, whose teachings resonate with a more-than-human wisdom, and whose life shines with a consistency and brilliance which intrigues all who observe it? Can one discredit the man's own understanding of his origins, insisting instead upon a naturalistic explanation for that man's totally unique life?

First, the question of the authenticity of the gospel records must be settled. Is Jesus just a legend, the figment of fertile imaginations? We discussed this question briefly at the beginning of our study primarily to "clear some room for ourselves to get on with the investigation." Hopefully, your own exposure to the gospel records as a "reasonable starting point in our quest" has brought you to the conclusion that the records are authentic. If we grant the gospel records the same neutral respect we grant all other historical documents, and if we submit them to the same validity tests we submit all other documents, the substantial correctness of the gospel narrative is beyond reasonable doubt, and the likelihood of Jesus being merely a legend is beyond reason.

At the risk of being redundant, "Let us suppose, for a moment, that the four Gospels have no existence; and let us suppose the problem [is] given us to construct, by the aid of sheer imagination, a history which would correspond in its minuteness with that given in the Gospels, and throughout consistently exhibit the daily life of one making such exalted claims, and acting in accordance with them. Who would not pronounce the task to be impossible? Yet, such a history exists; and the mere fact of its existence is sufficient vindication of its truth. The picture of the life and character of Jesus, exhibited in the Gospels with the utmost minuteness and variety of detail . . . accords most fully with the claims he is represented as advancing."[2] Philip Schaff concurs:

> A character so original, so complete, so uniformly consistent, so perfect, so human and yet so high above all human greatness, can be neither a fraud nor a fiction. . . . It would take more than a Jesus to invent a Jesus."[3]

As Fosdick affirmed, "The personality of Jesus, as portrayed in the Gospels, is so vivid, his individual characteristics are so lively and unmistakable, he stands out so distinctively himself and not anyone else, that the story leaves the intense impression of a real man, dealing with real people, in an actual historic situation."[4]

If we accept the Gospels as authentic records of a real man dealing with real people, we are pressed to answer yet another question: Was Jesus lying when he made claims to deity? Philip Schaff answers pointedly:

> How, in the name of logic, common sense, and experience, could an imposter — that is a deceitful, selfish, depraved man — have invented, and consistently maintained from the beginning to end, the purest and noblest character known in history with the most perfect air of truth and reality? How could he have conceived and successfully carried out a plan of unparalleled beneficence, moral magnitude, and sublimity, and sacrificed his own life for it, in the face of the strongest prejudices of his people and age?"[5]

Schaff states unequivocably, "Christ stands . . . alone among all the heroes of history, and presents to us an insolvable problem, unless we admit him to be more than man, even the eternal Son of God."[6]

But what Schaff thinks about Jesus doesn't matter. What I think about him doesn't matter. What *you* think about him does. From what you have learned — if only from this study — what is your assessment of him? Do you sense anything about him that would cause you to draw the conclusion that he was a liar? What impression have you received as to his truthfulness? Was he an honest man? You'll have to answer these questions for yourself.

But even if your impression is that Jesus was an honest man you must ask yet other questions: Was he honest — but honestly mistaken — about who he was? And if he was mistaken, does that necessarily mean he was a lunatic? In his claim to be God, could not Jesus have been unintentionally wrong and yet still sane? C. S. Lewis recognized the dilemma and addressed it in one of his most often-quoted passages:

> I am trying here to prevent anyone saying the really foolish thing that people often say about Him: "I'm ready to accept Jesus as the great moral teacher, but I don't accept His claim to be God." That is the one thing we must not say. A man who was merely a man and said the sort of things Jesus said would not be a great moral teacher. He would either be a lunatic — on the level with the man who says he is a poached egg — or else he would be the Devil of Hell. You must make your choice. Either this man was, and is, the Son of God; or else a madman or something worse. You can shut him up for a fool, you can spit at him and kill him as a demon; or you can fall at

his feet and call him Lord and God. But let us not come with any
patronizing nonsense about His being a great human teacher. He
has not left that open to us. He did not intend to.

It is possible, in regard to thousands of topics, to be
sincere, wrong and sane — all at the same time. A person can
be completely sincere in adding a column of figures, but totally
incorrect in his answer, and yet be considered altogether sane.
Mathematics is one of those areas in which this is not only
possible but prevalent.

However, in regard to one's perception of his personal
identity, society generally views as insane one who goes
around claiming to be God. And without question, Jesus did
claim to be God. D. S. Talcott, in the Boston Lectures of 1871,[7]
observed that the claims of Jesus "are so intimately interwoven with the whole tenor of his teachings, that, admitting
what no criticism calls in question, we can stop nowhere short
of the admission that Jesus claimed divine honors for
himself." Talcott further presses the issue by disqualifying the
supposition that Jesus was "under the control of an innocent
self-delusion":

> If there ever was a sound human intellect, clear, well-balanced, and
> raised above every influence that could disturb or cloud its opera-
> tion, it was the intellect displayed in the recorded life of Jesus of
> Nazareth. The only alternative that remains to us is, either to ac-
> cept him for what he declared himself to be, or to ascribe him, with-
> out any qualification, the boldest, the most arrogant, the most blas-
> phemous, of all impostures, yet an imposture steadily directed to
> the promotion of the highest style of goodness.[8]

To write off Jesus as deceived is as defenseless as attempting to convict him as a deceiver. On the one hand we are
presented with ignorant self-delusion; on the other wilful
deception. To put forward either as the explanation of the
"sublimest character ever recorded in history, and the foundation of the purest and most powerful system of ethics known to
man"[9] is irresponsible. "Since all four Gospels bristle with
supernatural claims on the part of Jesus . . . the person who
takes this position has surely not read the Gospels."[10] Strauss,
the strident critic/admirer of Jesus, gives every impression of
having read the Gospels thoroughly, and he agrees:

According to the first three Gospels, he knew God as his Father and God's affairs as his own. . . . According to John, he articulated positively his unity with the Father and presented himself as the visible revelation of him. In any case according to both representations this was neither a mere feigning nor a transient surge of Jesus' feeling in single heightened moments; rather his entire life and all his sayings and actions were permeated with this consciousness as from the soul.[11]

What is your impression of Jesus? Do *you* think he was insane?

In answering that question it may help you to consider one further thought: At the same time Jesus stands as "Earth's No. 1 Son" (H. G. Wells placed him at the top of his list of history's Ten Greatest Men.[12]) he was a man who had no consciousness of sin. He seemingly felt no need ever to repent. That fact, in and of itself, is not unique among humans. Others such as the simple-minded and sociopaths, often demonstrate no awareness of sin. They either were born with no capacity or have destroyed their conscience regarding sin. But Jesus fits neither category. Certainly not the category of the simple-minded; his teachings comprise the ultimate standard of ethical conduct. And certainly not that of a socio-path, such as a Hitler; Jesus' life was the epitome of moral excellence.

Yet, repentance for wrongdoing and moral inadequacy is the invariable beginning of all human goodness, and the noblest men are those most conscious of their human imperfections. It has always been true that a keen sense of wrong has been consistently the basis of the appreciation of the right.[13] "Yet, Christ, whose very presence stirs the consciousness of unworthiness in others, never Himself repents, never seems to regret word, thought, or deed, betrays no passing shadow or sense of wrong, inadequacy or failure. He confidently claims to have lived a life that glorifies God Himself. With the stern and hostile faces of those who sought his life ringled around Him He could ask: 'Which of you can point to sin in me?' None picked up the challenge in exultation, none dared to speak and say that such a question in itself was a piece of arrogant self-righteousness, which marked the fundamental of all sins — a damning pride. In him it did not seem arrogant."[14]

Is it possible that Jesus could be who he so often and so consistently claimed to be? Is it possible that in the presence and personality of Jesus we are confronted with God himself? This was the astonishing claim Jesus made. Taking into consideration Jesus' life, his teachings, his deeds and his claims, each person must decide whether Jesus was 1) a legend — the figment of someone's or some group's imagination; 2) a liar — one who intentionally deceived; 3) a lunatic — one who was honest but honestly mistaken; or 4) Lord. It is possible he was any one of these. Who do you think he *probably* was?

"So far as we are able to understand personality at all," observed C. H. Dodd, "we can see that the attitude of Jesus to God and to life, as portrayed in the Gospels, differs from our own and from that of other men precisely in its wholeness, simplicity, and finality. It is undisturbed as ours never is. [And] the effect he produced upon men with whom He came in contact — the effect indeed which He still produces upon men — is such that we cannot think He had any unresolved discords in His own soul.

"Thus while we do not uncritically accept what Jesus said because of a prior belief in His 'sinlessness,' yet there is something in the record that leads us to believe that in some deep and not fully explicable way His inner life possessed a unique moral perfection, which would account for the unique authority His words have actually carried in spite of all local and temporal limitations. It is ultimately this elusive personal 'something' that drives us back again and again to the . . . record of his words, to exhaust every resource of criticism in the attempt to recover the most authentic and original form of His teaching and to understand it as He meant it. And the more deeply we study the record the more sure do we become that behind all, even the most primitive, interpretation and application of His words, in the words themselves, lay a unique gift to men from the very Spirit of truth."[15]

The elusive "something" is what D. M. Baillie identified as Jesus' "personality, His character, His outlook, His attitude to life and God and man, His 'spiritual pilgrimage,' His obedience unto death, His victory, . . . His 'inner life.' "[16] This is the kind of historical element on which faith ultimately depends today. In our quest for a solid faith we are not limited to a cold and impersonal listing of facts which commend themselves to us without cost or consequence. We are confronted with a living Personality who commends Himself to us at all cost to Himself and calls for a personal response of faith with all its consequence to us. This elusive "something" is perhaps what Jesus meant when he said, ". . . everyone who *sees* the Son and believes in him [shall] have eternal life; and I will raise him up at the last day" (John 6:30).

We began this search by using the figure of a spelunker searching the unknown, not fearing where truth might bring us out. At least that is what was recommended as the safest course to pursue in a matter as serious as the one at hand. But it should not be assumed that everyone has followed that recommendation; and for one sobering reason: No human inherently wants a God — not God with a capital G who has authority over life. The human predicament stems precisely from the fact that humans want to be their own god, controlling their own life, doing what pleases themselves, not what pleases an Other. That's just the way we humans are.

Muggeridge concurred. He openly answered the question, "Is there a God?" with this frank confession:

> I myself should be very happy to answer with an emphatic negative. Temperamentally, it would suit me well enough to settle for what this world offers, and to write off as wishful thinking . . . any notion of a divine purpose and a divinity to intertain and execute it. . . . I have never wanted a God, or feared a God, or felt under any necessity to invent one.[17]

C. S. Lewis expressed the same reluctance: "I had always wanted, above all things, not to be 'interfered with'. I had wanted . . . 'to call my soul my own.' " He then shared with his readers this intimate moment:

> You must picture me alone in that room in Magdalen, night after night, feeling, whenever my mind lifted even for a second from my work, the steady unrelenting approach of Him whom I desired so earnestly not to meet. That which I greatly feared had at last come upon me. In the Trinity term of 1929 I gave in, and admitted that God was God, and knelt and prayed: perhaps, that night, the most dejected and reluctant convert in all England. I did not then see what is now the most shining and obvious thing; the Divine humility which will accept a convert even on such terms. The Prodigal Son at least walked home on his own feet. But who can duly adore that Love which will open the high gates to a prodigal who is brought in kicking, struggling, resentful, and darting his eyes in every direction for a chance of escape.[18]

It is this one fact — that we do not want a God — that may cause an otherwise logical person to conclude that, in spite of all the evidence regarding the existence of God and the identity of Jesus, there is no God and that Jesus was wrong in his claims.

One day I sat in the home of a man in New Zealand and reasoned with him about the things we have been considering. He became defensive and said, "I don't need a God. I love my family; I treat my neighbor right; I don't lie or cheat or steal . . ." So he stated his case for not needing a God. He presented as evidence those things he considered to be of value; principles he would not be willing to live without; ethics upon which was founded the society that had given him birth and nourishment. Without realizing the implications of his answer, he had cited the Judeo-Christian ethic as evidence that he did not need a God.

I said, "Where did you obtain the ethical standards you have just cited, which you hold essential to life? They came from the very God of whom you say you have no need."

Then I said, "Let's set aside our attempts to prove or disprove God. For the sake of argument let's say we do not know."

"But if there were a God," I asked, "would it be your desire to serve him?" The man didn't answer.

But this is where the issue finally will be settled. The evidence is sufficient for us to draw a satisfactory conclusion — one we can live with . . . and die for. Are we willing to accept someone with complete authority over our lives? It is this issue Jesus addressed when he said, "If any man is willing to do God's will he shall know whether the teaching is from God or whether I am speaking on my own authority" (John 7:17). "If any man is willing . . . he shall know . . ." Until one has settled the issue of the human will one is not prepared to draw a conclusion about Jesus.

John Baillie admits, "I do know that in fact it is the constraint of Jesus Christ from which I find it most impossible to escape. I just cannot read the Gospel story without knowing that I am being sought out in love, that I am at the same time being called to life's most sacred task and being offered life's highest prize. For it is the love God has shown me in Christ that constrains me to the love of my fellow man. If there be someone who is aware of no such constraint, I cannot, of course, hope to make him aware of it by speaking these few sentences. That would require, not so much a more elaborate argument as something quite different from any argument. But I am not now arguing. I am only confessing.''[19]

I have been drawn by that same power. Some twenty years ago I made an intense, nine-month investigation of the life of Jesus. At the conclusion of the investigation I came to the conviction that if, by some strange twist, following Jesus of Nazareth should mean I would die and go to Hell, if he is there also, I would not object to being in Hell. In fact, I would not want to be anywhere else. I concluded that, based on what I had seen in Jesus, I did not want to be anywhere he was not.

Does such a conclusion seem emotional and irrational? It might at first. But think for a moment: Would you want to spend a lifetime (to say nothing of eternity) in an environment where all that Jesus taught and lived for was outlawed and where he was not allowed to be? I wouldn't — not for all the gold in Fort Knox! And, at this point in our quest, I must say "I am not now arguing, I am only confessing."

And you? Based on what you have learned about Jesus in this investigation, what conclusion have you drawn? Ironically, due largely to the influence Jesus has had on the society in which you live, you are free to examine the evidence for yourself and draw your own conclusion.

Free to examine and choose, but, as with any choice, not free of the consequences of the choice.

1. L. P. Jacks, as quoted by D. M. Baillie, Op. cit., p. 102.

2. D. S. Talcott, "Jesus Christ Himself The All-Sufficient Evidence of Christianity," in *Christianity and Skepticism* (Boston: Congregational Publishing Society, 1871), pp. 413, 414.

3. Philip Schaff, *History of the Christian Church* (Grand Rapids: William B. Eerdmans Publishing Co., 1962), p. 109.

4. Fosdick, Op. cit., p. 17.

5. Philip Schaff, *The Person of Christ* (New York: Charles Scribner's Sons, 1882), p. 103.

6. Ibid., p. 30.

7. Talcott, Op. cit., p. 407.

8. Ibid.

9. Ballard, Op. cit., p. 261.

10. Trueblood, Op. cit., p. 41.

11. Strauss, Op. cit., p. 800.

12. Wells, Op. cit.

13. Ballard, Op. cit., p. 263.

14. Blaiklock, Op. cit., p. 75.

15. C. H. Dodd, *The Authority of the Bible* (Great Britain: Collins Press/Fontana Books, 1929), p. 226.

16. D. M. Baillie, *Faith in God* (London: Faber and Faber, n.d.), p. 251.

17. Muggeridge, Op. cit., p. 83.

18. C. S. Lewis, *Surprised By Joy* (London: Geoffrey Bles, 1955), pp. 214, 215.

19. John Baillie, *A Reasoned Faith* (New York: Charles Scribner's Sons, 1963), pp. 118, 119.

12

Conclusion

J. Wallace Hamilton[1] tells of two officers of the Russian Air Force who flew their plane to a neutral zone, asked for asylum in America and lived here for a while. But after a year or two one of them could not take it any more. He turned himself in to the Russian authorities, and they sent him back to Russia. The other who stayed in America wrote an article for a magazine explaining why. The article was entitled, "Freedom Frightens Me." He said his friend went back to Russia because he could not face the exacting demands of freedom. Mr. Hamilton observed that the man's return to a state of semi-slavery was "a most illuminating revelation of what happens in the human soul when the religious basis of civilization is abandoned and the light of God is blown out." Accustomed all his life to having his choices made for him, he could not make his own. He was a lost soul in the frightening atmosphere of freedom. "In other words," noted Hamilton, "he was unfitted to be a man."

Many who read this book will have come out of religious, or non-religious, backgrounds almost as rigid as that of the Russian pilots. Accustomed all their lives to having their choices made for them by others, they find themselves hard pressed to make their own. Some will reach down and find the courage to launch out in faith and make the decision to walk into the freedom which is the inalienable right of every human

173

being. Others will shrink back into the familiar state of religious (or irreligious) semi-slavery, preferring to have others
make their decisions for them. In so doing, they fail one of the
tests of life.

As we come to the end of this search, I hope you think long
and hard before you renounce your heritage as a human being
— the freedom to live responsibly before God. It is a "bit of the
infinite dignity [God] possesses in Himself [and has] bestowed
upon a human being."[2] Freedom — this likeness of God in ourselves — is risky business but a gift of inestimable value. As
you contemplate the decision which each person must make for
himself or herself, realize that the freedom you have been given
to act responsibly upon your convictions is an exercise of
God's nature stamped indelibly in your nature. "Live free or
die" incurs risk . . . and danger, but it also leads to dignity
and fullness of life. Edward Markham wrote about the
dilemma and the destiny involved in such a path:

> When in the dim beginning of the years,
> God mixed in man the raptures and the tears
> And scattered through his brain the starry stuff,
> He said, "Behold! yet this is not enough,
> For I must test his spirit to make sure
> That he can dare the vision and endure.
>
> I will withdraw my Face,
> Veil me in shadow for a certain space,
> Leaving behind Me only a broken clue —
> A crevice where the glory glimmers through,
> Some whisper from the sky,
> Some footprint in the road to track Me by;
>
> I will leave man to make the fateful guess,
> Will leave him torn between the No and Yes,
> Leave him unresting till he rests in Me,
> Drawn upward by the choice that makes him free —
> Leave him in the tragic loneliness to choose,
> With all in life to win or all to lose.[3]

---

1. J. Wallace Hamilton, *Who Goes There* (Fleming H. Revel Company,
1958), pp. 79, 80.

2. Ibid., p. 78.

3. Edward Markham, "The Testing," as quoted by J. Wallace Hamilton
in *Who Goes There*, Op. cit., pp. 79, 80.

BIBLIOGRAPHY

Anders, Dan. "Profile of a Christian," *We Preach Christ Crucified*. Malibu, CA: Pepperdine University Press, 1986.

Baillie, D. M. *Faith in God*. London: Faber and Faber, n.d.

Baillie, John. *A Reasoned Faith*. New York: Charles Scribner's Sons, 1963.

Ballard, Frank. *The Miracles of Unbelief*. Edinburg: T. & T. Clark, 1900.

Barnette, Henlee H. *Introducing Christian Ethics*. Nashville, TN: Broadman Press, 1961.

Beaverbrook, Lord. *The Divine Propagandist*. London: Heinemann, 1962.

Becker, Carl L. "The Last Judgment," as quoted in *The Practical Cogitator*. Boston: Houghton Mifflin Company, 1945.

Blaiklock, E. M. *Who Was Jesus?* Chicago: Moody Press, 1974.

Boulter, Cedric. "Heinrich Schliemann," *Academic American Encyclopedia*. Danbury, Conn.: Grolier Incorporated, 1984.

Brougher, James Whitcomb. *Life and Laughter*. Valley Forge: The Judson Press, 1950.

Bruce, F. F. *The New Testament Documents: Are They Reliable?* Downers Grove, Ill.: Intervarsity Press, 1964.

Buscaglia, Leo F. *Personhood*. New York: Fawcett Columbine, 1978.

Christi, Marian. "Leo Buscaglia: 'Dr. Hug'," *Boston Globe*, Oct. 21, 1984, Sec. B, pp. 15, 19.

"Christmas Gift." *Time*, Dec. 30, 1985, p. 71, col. 3.

Daniel-Rops. *Jesus and His Times*, vol. I. Garden City, N.Y.: Image Books, 1958.

Dodd, C. H. *The Authority of the Bible*. Great Britain: Collins Press/Fontana Books, 1929.

Dorpfeld, Wilhelm. *Troja and Ilion*. (Athens, Greece, 1902), as quoted by Wood: *In Search of the Trojan War*.

Doyle, James J. "Writing Couple Believes World in Decline Peril," *Memphis Commercial Appeal*, Dec. 4, 1977, Sec. C, p. 6.

Durant, Will. "Caesar and Christ," in *The Story of Civilization, vol. 3*. New York: Simon and Schuster, 1944, p. 557.

Erwin, Gayle. *The Jesus Style*. Waco, TX: Word Publishers, 1986.

Fitch, Robert E. *Of Love and Suffering*. Philadelphia: The Westminster Press, n.d.

Fosdick, Harry Emerson. *The Man From Nazareth*. New York: Harper and Brothers, 1949.

Frankl, Victor. *Man's Search For Meaning*. New York: Washington Square Press, 1959.

Fromm, Erich. *The Art of Loving*. New York: Bantam Books, 1956.

Gavron, Daniel. *Walking through Israel*. Boston: Houghton Mifflin Company, 1980.

Gay, Peter. *The Enlightenment, An Interpretation*. New York: Vintage Books/Random House, 1968.

Geering, Lloyd. *God In The New World*. Great Britain, Hodder and Stoughton, 1968.

Geisler, Norman. "The Collapse of Modern Atheism," *The Intellectuals Speak Out About God*. Regnery Gateway, Inc., 1984.

Glasgall, Bill. "On the Cheap: The Unhappy Life of J. Paul Getty" *Business Week*, 21 April, 1986.

Globe Magazine. July 1, 1986.

Glover, T. R. *The Jesus of History*. London: Hodder and Stoughton, 1965 edition.

Goethe. "On Immortality," as quoted in *The Practical Cogitator*. Boston: Houghton Mifflin Company, 1945.

Guinness, Os. *The Dust of Death*. London: InterVarsity Press, 1973.

Hamilton, J. Wallace. *Who Goes There?*. Fleming H. Revel Company, 1958.

Harcack, Adolph. *What Is Christianity?* New York: Harper and Brothers, 1957.

Hatfield, Mark. *Between a Rock and a Hard Place*. Waco, TX: Word Books, 1976.

Henninger, Lanny. "Who Cares For The Children?" *We Preach Christ Crucified*. Malibu, CA: Pepperdine University Press, 1986.

Henson, H. H. *Christian Morality*. Oxford: Clarendon Press, 1936.

Hubbell, John G. *Reader's Digest*. August, 1986.

Hughes, T. P. quoted by Frank Ballard. *The Miracles of Unbelief*. Edinburg: T. & T. Clark, 1900.

Huxley, T. H. "Letter to Kingsley," as quoted in *The Practical Cogitator*. Boston: Houghton Mifflin Company, 1945.

Iacocca, Lee. *Iacocca, An Autobiography*. New York: Bantom Books, 1984.

Jaki, Stanley L. "Science: From the Womb of Religion," *The Christian Century*.

James, Will. "Pragmatism," as quoted in *The Practical Cogitator. Essays in Radical Empiricism*. Cambridge, Mass: Harvard University Press, 1976.

Josephus. *Wars.* William Whiston, trans. Philadelphia: The John C. Winston Company, n.d. *Antiquities,* XVII. 10. 5, p. 523.

Keller, Werner. *The Bible as History.* London: Hodder and Stoughton, 1956.

Kierkegaard, S. *Concluding Unscientific Postscript.* Princeton: Princeton University Press, 1944.

Kingman, Harry. "Mohti, One of the Immortals," *Unity.*

Klausner, Joseph. *Jesus of Nazareth.* New York: Macmillan Co., 1925.

Kubler-Ross, Elisabeth. *On Death and Dying.* New York: Macmillan Publishing Co., 1969.

Larson, Bruce. *The Relational Revolution.* Waco, TX: Word Books, 1976.

Lewis, C. S. *Surprised By Joy.* London: Geoffrey Bles, 1955.

Lewis, C. S. *Mere Christianity.* New York: The Macmillan Company, 1943.

Lewis, C. S. "Man or Rabbit?," *God In The Dock.* Grand Rapids: William B. Eerdmans Publishing Co., 1970.

Lewis, Ralph L. and Gregg. *Inductive Preaching.* Westchester, Ill., Crossway Books, 1983.

Lofthouse, W. F. "Biblical Ethics." *A Companion to the Bible,* 1st edition. Edinburgh: T. & T. Clark, 1936.

Machen, J. Greshem. *Christianity and Liberalism.* Grand Rapids: Wm. B. Eerdmans Publishing Co., 1946.

Maltz, Maxwell M.D. *Psycho-Cybernetics.* New York: Pocket Books/Simon and Schuster, Inc., 1960.

McCormick, Jay. "Investors Find Faith, Dow Up 29," *USA Today,* 28 May, 1986, Sec. B, p. 1.

McDowell, Josh. *More Than A Carpenter.* Wheaton, Ill.: Living Books, 1985.

McGinnis, Alan Loy. *Bringing Out The Best In People.* Minneapolis: Augsburg Publishing House, 1985.

Menninger, Karl. *Love Against Hate.* New York: Harcourt, Brace & World, Inc., 1942.

Merton, Thomas. *The Power and Meaning of Love.* New York: Farrar, Straus & Cudahy, 1980.

Miller, Randolph Crump. *Living With Anxiety.* Philadelphia: Pilgrim Press, 1971.

Muggeridge, Malcolm. *Chronicles of Wasted Time,* Vol. I, "The Green Stick." New York: William Morrow & Co., 1973.

Muggeridge, Malcolm. "Another King," *Jesus Rediscovered.* New York: Doubleday & Company, Inc., 1969.

Nedoncelle, Maurice. *Love and the Person.* New York: Sheed and Ward, 1986.

Ogden, Schubert M. *The Reality of God.* New York, Harper & Row, 1963.

Olds, Charles Burnell. *Love: The Issue.* Boston: The Christopher Publishing House, n.d.

Peale, Norman Vincent. *The Power of Positive Thinking.* Greenwich, Conn.: Fawcett Publications, 1952.

Peale, Norman Vincent. *The Art of Real Happiness.* New York: Prentice Hall, Inc., 1950.

Phillips, Gerard. *The Church in the Modern World,* as quoted by James J. Kavanaugh, *Struggle of the Unbeliever.* New York: Trident Press, 1967.

Phillips, J. B. *Ring of Truth.* London: Hodder and Stoughton, 1967.

Pool, Lynn and Gray. *One Passion, Two Loves.* New York: Thomas Y. Crowell Company, 1966.

Ramsey, Sir William. *The Bearing of Recent Discovery on the Trustworthiness of the New Testament.* London: Hodder and Stoughton, 1915.

Reader's Digest, October, 1952.

Rosen, Moishe. *Jews For Jesus.* Old Tappan, New Jersey: Fleming H. Revell Company, 1946.

Russell, Bertrand. *Why I Am Not A Christian and Other Essays.* London: George Allen & Unwin Ltd., 1957.

Russell, Bertrand. *Has Man A Future?.* Harmondsworth: Penguin Books, 1961.

Sacred Books and Literature of the East, "Hymns To The One Universal God." New York: Parke, Austin, and Lipscomb, Inc., 1917.

Saunders, Landon. "Working Paper," unpublished, p. 45.

Schaeffer, Frances. *The God Who Is There.* Downers Grove, Ill.: University Press, 1968.

Schaeffer, Francis A. *How Should We Then Live?* Crossway Books, Westchester, Ill., 1976.

Schaff, Philip. *History of the Christian Church.* Grand Rapids: William B. Eerdmans Publishing Co., 1962.

Schaff, Philip. *The Person of Christ.* New York: Charles Scribner's Sons, 1882.

Schonfield, Hugh J. *The Passover Plot.* New York: Bernard Geis Associates, 1965.

Sorokin, Pitirim A. "Love, Its Aspects," *Explorations of Altruistic Love and Behavior.* Boston: Beacon Press, 1950.

Spinka, Matthew. *Christian Thought From Erasmus to Berdyaev.* Prentice-Hall, Inc., Englewood Cliffs, N.J., 1962.

Spitz, Rene A. "Hospitalism: An Inquiry Into the Genesis of Psychiatric Conditions in Early Childhood" in R. S. Eissler et al. (eds.). *Psychoanalytic Study of the Child,* Vol. 1. New York: International Universities Press, 1945 and "Hospitalism: A Follow-up Report," *Psychoanalytic Study of the Child,* vol. 2. New York: International Universities Press, 1946.

Stone, Irving. *The Greek Treasure.* New York: Doubleday & Company, 1975.

Strauss, David Friedrich. *The Life of Jesus Critically Examined*. Philadelphia: Fortress Press, 1972.

Talcott, D. S. "Jesus Christ Himself The All-Sufficient Evidence of Christianity," in *Christianity and Skepticism*. Boston: Congregational Publishing Society, 1871.

Teachings of The Compassionate Buddha, New York: Mentor Books, 1955.

Tillich, Paul. *Theology of Culture*. New York: Oxford University Press, 1964.

Trueblood, Elton. *A Place To Stand*. New York: Harper and Row, 1969.

Trueblood, Elton. *The Humor of Christ*. New York: Harper and Row, 1964.

Trueblood, D. Elton. *The Predicament of Modern Man*. New York: Harper Brothers, 1944.

Turner, H. E. W. "The Life and Teachings of Jesus Christ," *A Companion to the Bible*, 2nd edit. Edinburgh: T. & T. Clark, 1963.

Van Kamm, Adrian. *Religion and Personality*. Garden City, N.Y.: Image Books/Doubleday & Company, Inc., 1968.

Weigle, Luther. *Jesus and the Educational Method*. New York: Abingdon Press, 1939.

Wendt, Hans Heinrich. *The Teachings of Jesus*. New York: Charles Scribner's Sons, 1899.

Williams, David Rhys. *World Religions and the Hope for Peace*. Boston: The Beacon Press, 1951.

Wood, Michael. *In Search of the Trojan War*. New York: New American Library, Plume Books, 1985.

World Council of Churches. "Man's Disorder and God's Design," vol. 2: *The Church's Witness To God's Design*, The Amsterdam Assembly Series. New York: Harper and Brothers, 1948.

*The Rock which the builders rejected
has become the cornerstone...*

— *Jesus (ca. A.D. 30).*